If Not Now,

When?

Another Storm is brewing

By Linwood S. Hancock

A Call to Revolution
For the Evolution
Of Black People

Bloomington, IN   Milton Keynes, UK

authorHOUSE

AuthorHouse™
1663 Liberty Drive, Suite 200
Bloomington, IN 47403
www.authorhouse.com
Phone: 1-800-839-8640

AuthorHouse™ UK Ltd.
500 Avebury Boulevard
Central Milton Keynes, MK9 2BE
www.authorhouse.co.uk
Phone: 08001974150

© 2007 Linwood S. Hancock. All rights reserved.

No part of this book may be reproduced, stored in a retrieval system, or transmitted by any means without the written permission of the author.

First published by AuthorHouse 1/25/2007

ISBN: 978-1-4259-8679-7 (sc)

Library of Congress Control Number: 2007900330

Printed in the United States of America
Bloomington, Indiana

This book is printed on acid-free paper.

What is it that we need to survive everyday that we (Black People) produce, besides entertainment, funeral services and skin care?

Considering all of the wealth and consumer power we possess; how many jobs and career opportunities do we (Black People) provide for our own people?

How do we protect and improve our communities and the lives of our children when we don't even control the politics, educational systems or businesses within our own communities?

In Loving Memory Of Radee

This book is dedicated to my family

To my beloved Father who sheltered, disciplined, and nurtured me – God Rest His Soul
To my adored Mother who's lessons I will carry with me forever – Still the Matriarch
To my older Brothers, Butch and Zac – I hope you have found peace in the Lord's House
To my baby Sister Desiree – I am very proud of you and your dedication to family
To all of my children – Linwood III, Monica & Monique, Miles, Jordyn, Radee and Fatia

And last, but not least
To my loving and supportive Wife Evelyn -
who has helped me to free my spirit so that it can soar with the eagles.

Letter To My Readers

My name is Linwood S. Hancock II and I am simply a Black American who has survived through many of the different phases of the Black American Experience. I am not a scholar nor am I a civic leader, religious leader or politician. I also do not hold any political affiliations. I am simply a Black man in America. I do not write with the eloquence of people like W.E.B. Dubois, Langston Hughes, Cornell West and others like them. I write for and to the common man and woman; men and women like me. People who have worked hard in this country, fought for this country, and supported this country for most, if not all of their lives.

Because of the fact that I am not an academic or scholar, I express myself in 'grass-root' terms. I speak and write to and from the common man's perspective. I am virtually self-taught in my journey to learn and master myself. My true beginnings and origin shape who I am today. My hunger and desire to learn about myself is not for riches, but simply for the pursuit of truth, honesty and integrity for my people and myself. I long for brotherhood, empathy and community amongst my people who live in all aspects of American life. Also, I long to connect with my people all over the world.

Throughout this book, I use quotes and passages from books written years ago. There is a distinct reason for that. The reason is to show that the problems and sufferings that we endured as a people over one hundred years ago, still plague us today. In other words, most of the progress that we have made is, for the most part, only on the surface. The authors of many of the books that I have cited have all died many years ago and bore no witness or knowledge of our struggles of today. However, their views and visions, when put in the context of today's society, speak directly to our present-day condition.

The effect that I am trying to reveal is that we have not progressed that much at all from the days of Reconstruction and the abolition of slavery. During those early days of our new freedom we created large communities, held high office in government, became doctors, lawyers, entrepreneurs and business men and women. Back then, although we created and supported large communities, we could not defend those communities. Today, over one hundred years later, we still cannot defend our communities, let alone define them.

Today, we still do not own 'life-sustaining' businesses that would help us survive independently. We are not organized or strong enough to form alliances that would help in the defense of our human rights or communities. We must remember that the first blood spilled in the war for the independence of this country was the blood of a Black man named Crispus Attucks!! When will we be prepared to spill blood (whether literally or symbolically) for our own independence? Today, we can begin to change the definition of the Black American. Today, we can begin to change the definition of the Black man all over the world. America is not a white country. Although it is ruled by white leaders, this country has always been inhabited by people of color. As it was before they got here, when the work needed to be done, and even more so today.

This book represents my search of the anti-venom that will reverse the effects of that venomous snakebite called racism. The effects of racism and discrimination are still, today, coursing through our bloodstream and because there are no outward or surface wounds we sometimes tend to forget or even deny their presence or existence.

So I speak to the common man; for it is only through us that the necessary changes must originate. I am not angry at the white race; they did what they needed to do to survive in a world where they found themselves to be the minority. This book is not about slavery and what the white man did to us, rather it is about who and where we are now and what we need to do in order to change our state of being.

This book is designed to invoke controversy and conversation, to inspire movement and change and to instill self-pride and dignity to a once-great people now lost.

Linwood S. Hancock II

FOREWORD

"We will not be satisfied to take one jot or tittle less than our full manhood rights."
W.E.B. Dubois' Address to the Country
Second Annual Meeting of the Niagara Movement

The men of the Niagara Movement coming from the toil of the year's hard work and pausing a moment from the earning of their daily bread turn toward the nation and again ask in the name of ten million the privilege of a hearing. In the past year the work of the Negro hater has flourished in the land. Step by step the defenders of the rights of American citizens have retreated. The work of stealing the Black man's ballot has progressed and the fifty and more representatives of stolen votes still sit in the nation's capital. Discrimination in travel and public accommodation has so spread that some of our weaker brethren are actually afraid to thunder against color discrimination as such and are simply whispering for ordinary decencies.

Against this the Niagara Movement eternally protests. We will not be satisfied to take one jot or tittle less than our full manhood rights. We claim for ourselves every single right that belongs to a freeborn American, political, civil and social, and until we get these rights we will never cease to protest and assail the ears of America. The battle we wage is not for ourselves alone but for all true Americans. It is a fight for ideals, lest this, our common fatherland, false to its founding become in truth the land of the thief and the home of the Slave -a by-word and a hissing among the nations for its sounding pretensions and pitiful accomplishment.

Never before in the modern age has a great and civilized folk threatened to adopt so cowardly a creed in the treatment of its fellow-citizens born and bred on its soil. Stripped of verbiage and subterfuge and in its naked nastiness the new American creed says: Fear to let black men even try to rise lest they become the equals of the white. And this is the land that professes to follow Jesus Christ. The blasphemy of such a course is only matched by its cowardice.

In detail our demands are clear and unequivocal. First, we would vote; with the right to vote goes everything. Freedom, manhood, the honor of your wives, the chastity of your daughters, the right to work, and the chance to rise, and let no man listen to those who deny this. We want full manhood suffrage, and we want it now, henceforth and forever.

Second. We want discrimination in public accommodation to cease. Separation in railway and streetcars, based simply on race and color is un-American, un-democratic, and silly. We protest against all such discrimination.

Third. We claim the right of freemen to walk, talk, and be with them that wish to be with us. No man has a right to choose another man's friends, and to attempt to do so is an impudent interference with the most fundamental human privilege.

Fourth. We want the laws enforced against rich as well as poor, against Capitalist as well as Laborer, against white as well as black. We are not more lawless than the white race, we are more often arrested convicted, and mobbed. We want justice even for criminals and outlaws. We want the Constitution of the country enforced. We want Congress to take charge of Congressional elections. We want the Fourteenth amendment carried out to the letter and every State disfranchised in Congress, which attempts to disfranchise its rightful voters. We want Fifteenth amendment enforced and No State allowed to base its franchise simply on color.

The failure of the Republican Party in Congress at the session just closed to redeem its pledge of 1904 with reference to suffrage conditions at the South seems a plain, deliberate, and premeditated breach of promise, and stamps that party as guilty of obtaining votes under false pretense.

Fifth. We want our children educated. The school system in the country districts of the South is a disgrace and in few towns and cities are the Negro schools what they ought to be. We want the national government to step in and wipe out illiteracy in the South. Either the United States will destroy ignorance or ignorance will destroy the United States.

And when we call for education we mean real education. We believe in work. We ourselves are workers, but work is not necessarily education. Education is the development of power and ideal. We want our children trained as intelligent human beings should be, and we will fight for all time against any proposal to educate black boys and girls simply as servants and underlings, or simply for the use of other people. They have a right to know, to think, to aspire.

These are some of the chief things, which we want. How shall we get them? By voting where we may vote, by persistent, unceasing agitation; by hammering at the truth, by sacrifice and work.

We do not believe in violence, neither in the despised violence of the raid nor the lauded violence of the soldier, nor the barbarous violence of the mob, but we do believe in John Brown, in that incarnate spirit of justice, that hatred of a lie, that willingness to sacrifice money, reputation, and life itself on the altar of right. And here on the scene of John Brown's martyrdom we reconsecrate ourselves, our honor, our property to the final emancipation of the race which John Brown died to make free.

Our enemies, triumphant for the present, are fighting the stars in their courses. Justice and humanity must prevail. We live to tell these dark brothers of ours-scattered in counsel, wavering and weak-that no bribe of money or notoriety, no promise of wealth or fame, is worth the surrender of a people's manhood or the loss of a man's self-respect. We refuse to surrender the leadership of this race to cowards and trucklers. We are men; we will be treated as men. On this rock we have planted our banners. We will never give up, though the trump of doom find us still fighting.

And we shall win. The past promised it, the present foretells it. Thank God for John Brown! Thank God for Garrison and Douglass! Sumner and Phillips, Nat Turner and Robert Gould Shaw, and all the hallowed dead who died for freedom! Thank God for all those to-day, few though their voices be, who have not forgotten the divine brotherhood of all men white and black, rich and poor, fortunate and unfortunate.

We appeal to the young men and women of this nation, to those whose nostrils are not yet befouled by greed and snobbery and racial narrowness: Stand up for the right, prove yourselves worthy of your heritage and whether born north or south dare to treat men as men. Cannot the nation that has absorbed ten million foreigners into its political life without catastrophe absorb ten million Negro Americans into that same political life at less cost than their unjust and illegal exclusion will involve?

Courage brothers! The battle for humanity is not lost or losing. All across the skies sit signs of promise. The slave is raising in his might, the yellow millions are tasting liberty, the black Africans are writhing toward the light, and everywhere the laborer, with ballot in his hand, is voting open the gates of Opportunity and Peace. The morning breaks over blood-stained hills. We must not falter, we may not shrink. Above are the everlasting stars."
                W.E.B. Dubois, The Souls of Black Folk,
                Authoritative Text, Context and Criticism, 1999

INTRODUCTION

History has reminded us time and time again of our status here in this country and other parts of the world. Recent history has witnessed our people being enslaved, degraded, subjugated, experimented on, medically ignored and economically deprived. Although there have been those who have soared to great heights, we have yet to reach our potential as a people. Ancient history reflects our ancestors as being the greatest rulers and warriors to ever exist on this planet. World history, science, religion and archeology have taught us that we are the descendants of the originators of civilization, medicine, science, architecture, government, mathematics and even the spoken word. Despite such a rich origin, we are also the only people in history to have been stolen from our native land, stripped of culture, language, religion, murdered, castrated, lynched and otherwise subjugated and still survive. Yes, we are still here. Does this not speak of our strength and resolve? Do we, as a people, not recognize that in every phase of world civilization we have risen to the top? Whether in medicine, mathematics, science, the arts, sports, war and even in world diplomacy we have represented with excellence despite the treatment we have received.

The following words will serve as a challenge to all Black people all over the world, but especially here in the United States. We here in the U.S. have access to the greatest resources and wealth in the entire world. Yet, so few of us have taken advantage of those resources. I challenge all religious leaders, teachers, professors, men, women and especially parents to step up the pace. It is now the 21st Century and we are still receiving second-class treatment. It is now time to make dramatic change.

I
STATE OF BLACKNESS

Alas, another catastrophic event has occurred in this society to show evidence of who and where we are in this country. For months, maybe years, debates will rage regarding who was at fault in the delayed response to the devastating destruction of Hurricane Katrina. The raw truth is that there is no particular person to blame at all. It is all too easy to point fingers at President Bush, after all, he is in charge. Then there is the Director of FEMA and the Secretary of Homeland Defense whose respective positions were responsible for just such events. We can even turn up our noses at Condoleeza Rice, the BLACK Secretary of State for defending these people. But the truth is that none of them are truly the blame. Not one single person listed above had a hand in establishing the status of the Black man in America. I would think, as did many others, that if the deeply southern, impoverished, predominantly black city of New Orleans were more important and integral in the daily operations of our government and/or this society, that the response and recovery efforts would have been more expedient and efficient. Did you know that Rescue Squads all the way from Canada were among the first responders to the catastrophe? They arrived only hours after the initial impact with support helicopters (They must have been listening to the weather report). In a small, obscure article in the Atlanta Journal Constitution on October 28, 2005, page D2, the United States Secretary of Energy, Sam Bodman publicly thanked Canada for its rapid response. On Sunday, September 4, 2005 CNN.com reported that the oil-rich nation of Qatar had offered the United States $100 million in relief and humanitarian supplies for the victims of Hurricane Katrina. The initial response from the U.S. Government was a refusal of all offers. Many different nations offered assistance. According to the report, offers came from "India, Sri Lanka, Thailand and Indonesia, the four countries hardest hit by the December 26 Asian tsunami. The State Department said offers of help had been received from more than 50 countries, including: Australia, Armenia, Bahamas, Belgium, Canada, China, Cuba, Saudi Arabia, Russia and many, many more. The Mexican Navy offered to send ships, helicopters and amphibious vehicles. As of the Friday before this report no offers were accepted. Maybe if it was known for something more important than the Superdome, jambalaya or Bourbon St., or, if it were predominately white, it would have gotten faster attention. Those are just maybes. In an essay written for the book "The Covenant", written by Tavis Smiley, Robert D. Bullard, Ph.D., a Professor of Sociology and Director of the Environmental Justice Resource Center (EFRC) at Clark Atlanta University in Atlanta, Ga., had this to say;

> "Hurricane Katrina exposed the world to the naked reality of environmental racism. Environmental racism refers to any policy practice, or directive that differentially affects or disadvantages, (whether intended or unintended) individuals, groups or communities based on race or color. Environmental racism combines with public policies and industry practices to provide benefits for whites while shifting costs to people of color. Katrina presented in living color clear links among race, poverty, land use, environmental risk, and unequal protection. Poverty impacts health because it determines how many resources poor people have and defines the amount of environmental risks they will be exposed to in their immediate environment."

Dr. Bullard went on further to say;

> *"Environmental health problems related to environmental exposure were hot-button issues in New Orleans long before Katrina's floodwaters emptied out the city. New Orleans' location on the Mississippi river Industrial Corridor increased its vulnerability to environmental threats. Dozens of toxic "time bombs" along this chemical corridor-the 85-mile stretch from Baton Rouge to New Orleans – made "Cancer Alley" a major environmental justice battleground."*

Robert D. Bullard, Ph.D., (The Covenant, Tavis Smiley, 2005)

If our leaders knew of this 'environmental injustice', what exactly did we do about it? Better yet, what could we do about it?

The real truth is that we (Black people) are the true blame. From the preachers to the teachers, from the parents to the political leaders, we are all the blame. African Americans have a stamp of ownership on many major aspects of American life. New Orleans is one of the exclusive ones. Why did we not claim ownership prior to this occurrence and why are we not a major part of the rebuilding process? In the same token, why is the MLK Memorial Center in 11 million dollars disrepair. Who are we waiting for to make those repairs? With all of the money floating around the Metro Atlanta area (his place of origin), why haven't we as a people claimed ownership of that legacy? In an article in the Atlanta Journal Constitution on September 16, 2005 on page A17, Minister Louis Farrakhan stated that there is evidence that a 25 foot crater was created beneath the levees to divert flood water from the French Quarter to the poor black section of downtown New Orleans. If this were true or fabricated, did we demand or execute a full-scale investigation into this allegation?

There is no doubt whatsoever in any knowledgeable mind that we, as a people, were kidnapped and enslaved in America. Our oppressors established our race as less than second-class citizens. In fact, we were only considered one third human. For that, they must take the blame. In regards to our status today, we must take the blame, because although they started it, we have perpetuated it. We, as a people, have diligently lived up to every profile and stereotype that they have labeled us with. Walking through the streets of the ghetto is as dangerous as walking through a strange jungle full of man-eating animals. Urban and rural neighborhoods, right here in the United States, are as dirty and unsanitary as the poorest villages in some third-world countries. There has been much conjecture regarding the reasons why so many Black Americans accept and exist in such deplorable living conditions. In my opinion, any conjectures, other than the cold, hard truth, are only excuses. Yes, it is all too true that our ancestors were enslaved. They were stripped of their culture, language and trained like pets to hate themselves and accept less than desirable conditions. However, since that time several generations have produced able, intelligent and courageous leaders that have led our people up and out of slavery to where we are now. People like Harriet Tubbman, Frederick Douglas, Marcus Garvey, Adam Clayton Powell, Dr. Martin Luther King and Malcolm X and many more, had all forged great gains for Black people in America. Today, all those names are simply history lessons. We as a people have forgotten how to rally together for a just cause. Our leaders have forgotten how to lead. We have evolved into aimless individualists who thrive on the concept that "I got mine, now you get yours." Our (and I use the word loosely) 'leaders' of today are not the courageous revolutionaries who dedicated their lives and convictions to the cause. To the contrary, they are pop and rock stars who suck the resources from the communities they serve so that they can live in luxury in giant mansions, drive Rolls Royces and Bentleys and wear fine clothes and jewelry. All the while, their constituencies and followers drown in communities flooded with ignorance, violence and illiteracy. The conditions that Black people face in America have been cited over and over and over again, but citing them and repeating them is just like saying, "I don't want to work today," after you've already punched in. You are already there! Just like yesterday and just like tomorrow. If you don't <u>DO</u> anything to change your state of being, you will continue to deal with the same conditions day-in, day-out.

Now, please don't get me wrong, I realize that everyone is not built to excel. I also realize that there will always be a class system here in America. But, we as Black people in America have always held a status somewhat lower than the lower-class. Yes, we have representatives in the upper classes and greater representation in the

If Not Now, When?

middle-classes, but the masses remain in virtual poverty and we, as a people still have no real power.

Many of the leaders of yesterday were men and women of modest means and rose to prominence through example. They were men and women of the people; they were just like us. Today's leaders have separated themselves from us. They live in huge, multi-million dollar gated mansions. How do we as a people connect to these types of leaders? They do not act as though they are the Chieftains of great villages, willing to sacrifice their all for the betterment of their village. They are not willing to wage war against the enemies of their village. They do not lay judgment or penalty down upon those who violate the laws of their communities. They do not even attempt to lead their people to a promise land. So tell me, what do they do except collect tithes, sell records, do cameos in movies and live very large? The people that actually do the most for us do it quietly, modestly, with passion and little resource.

Let us take a moment to clear up a serious misconception that many of our young people have. Entertainers and star athletes are not leaders. They can be classified as role models (some good, some bad), but they are not leaders. This is not to say that they cannot become leaders, but their convictions and focuses would have to change drastically. It would be very difficult to seriously promote community awareness and upward mobility for your people and still create music and live lifestyles that downgrade and depict negative images of the same people that you are trying to motivate. Oh, you may gain followers, but which message are they trying to follow? A 'wanna-be-thug' who sells a million records and makes a million dollars does not automatically evolve into a leader of our community. What he or she automatically evolves into is a 'wanna-be-thug' who can now afford fancy lawyers so that he can go out and try to do some of the things that real thugs do. Nino Brown from the movie New Jack City gave out turkeys and toys to the people. Did that make him a leader in the community?

It seems that today's generation holds up people the likes of P-Diddy, Russell Simmons and Master P in the same esteem that my generation held in Huey Newton, Eldridge Cleaver, Angela Davis and Leroy Jones. Unfortunately, they have no one to compare to Malcolm X and Martin Luther King. Speaking of Martin, where are the descendants of one of the greatest orators and inspirational leaders of our time? Where are the many protégés and interns who followed him around and hung on his every word? It is all too apparent that his torch, along with Malcolm's was not passed on, they just simply burned out.

> *"Black political leadership reveals the tame and genteel face of the black middle class. The black dress suits with white shirts worn by Malcolm X and Martin Luther King, Jr., signified the seriousness of their deep commitment to black freedom, whereas today the expensive tailored suits of black politicians symbolize their personal success and individual achievement. Malcolm and Martin called for the realization that black people are somebodies with which America has to reckon, whereas black politicians tend to turn our attention to their somebodiness owing to their "making it" in America.*
>
> Cornell West, "Race Matters", 2001

Today's generation thrives on the conviction of individual achievement. Many of them enjoy the many luxuries that have been historically only afforded to White America. They appear to move seamlessly among their white counterparts basically because money talks. However, the moment those same counterparts do or say something to remind them that they are still black and still in America, no matter how much money they have, they are now ready to cry discrimination. Money has a way of making people feel that they are different from the masses. They begin to feel that they have been accepted by the ruling classes. The so-called state of financial freedom provides a false security that leaves them feeling invulnerable and apart, or above the sufferings of their people. There are many notable and infamous cases that confirm this. O.J. Simpson, in his 'hey-day', was once the pride of "White America". He was the best at what he did and there was no one that came close to doing it like him at that time. He was handsome, personable, had a great smile and caused no controversy. He was put on a pedestal. Ahh, he was living the 'life of Reilly'. All until that fateful day that he was accused of murdering his white wife Nicole Simpson and her friend Ronald Goldman. Now, it is time to cry racism. Oprah Winfrey, (whom I adore for her accomplishments), in all her glory, cried racism when an exclusive store would not open its closed doors so that she could pick up a few things. Danny Glover expressed frustration in the news when a New York cabbie would not stop for him. Folks, we go through this type of thing everyday. We just cannot call a press conference about it. It's just not newsworthy.

Now, I know that Oprah and Danny give tremendously to many causes for the Black experience, but most of us only see them on television; somewhere that many of us don't even dream of going. We don't see them in our communities. Too few, too quietly, come back to the inner-city schools and teaches our children in classes on economic achievement or self-pride. We see you on TV looking simply marvelous, getting better with age and living long healthy and prosperous lives. We can't begin to afford nutritionists, chefs and personal trainers. We don't see anyone with any 'juice' coming down here and pressuring the Board of Education to return Physical Education as a major course of study especially when high blood pressure, obesity and heart disease is killing us at a higher rate than anyone else. You may ask, "Why is this my responsibility?" The answer to that question is; it is not your responsibility. It is all of our responsibility. Each and every one of us should take up arms together against any of the things that subject our people to injustice or unequal treatment. The problem is simply that we, as a people, are a leaderless flock. It is human nature to follow and without a true leader, we wander aimlessly. The individuals that we do choose to follow are all moving in different directions or moving against each other. It seems that they all have separate agendas. It is very true that people like Oprah Winfrey, Danny Glover, Bill Cosby, Robert Johnson, Magic Johnson and Russell Simmons, to name a few, all contribute greatly to the cause. However, they are all contributing separately. With all of the individual power and position that we have accomplished; the super-successful lawyers and financial consultants, politicians and businessmen and women, why have we not come together to create a Black conglomerate so powerful that the world would have to stop and take notice. We need a mega-conglomerate that would take advantage of the fact that Black people, especially here in America, are one of the largest consumers and watch more television than anyone else in this nation.

We actually have individuals with great amounts of riches all over the world, hence, a conglomerate that would breach into the import/export of products; products that would rival the quality of Coca Cola and General Mills or Ford and Toyota. We have bolstered, supported and mastered the production of everything from automobiles to toilet paper; after all, we work in all of those plants. But how much of what we use daily do _We_ produce independently? How many real jobs are _We_ creating for our people?

Earlier I mentioned successful people coming into our communities and volunteering, or even working part-time as teachers and instructors in their specific field of study. Professionals like all of the lawyers, doctors, scientists, journalists, authors, financial analyst, stockbrokers, CEOs, public relations specialists, Human Resources professionals, actors, musicians and so on and so on are all needed. We need to critically address the areas of academics that we are lacking in our school systems. Mathematics, science, reading and writing all deserve special attention and our level of expectations should be raised to the ceiling. Failing should not be an option for our children nor ourselves. We need more scientists and journalists of the highest quality to represent our people and address the issues that are important to us. We need dedicated and fearless politicians and political science professionals who can maneuver within the political arenas with enough juice and savvy to make a difference, and all of them need our undaunted support.

I expect that the people whom I have named specifically here may think ill of me for using them as examples. For that I must apologize. But your names are the names people will recognize and I need people to be able to relate to what I am trying to say. I recognize, acknowledge, appreciate and applaud the many, many tremendous contributions that all of those named people have given.

II
BLACK PARENTING

I have asked a lot from people with money, influence and power. However, their efforts are not what it would take to start a New Revolution for the Evolution of Black people. The truth is that many of those people have been giving and giving for years only to make small dents in the kettle of problems that we endure as a people. The beginning of the Revolution for the Evolution of Black People must start in every Black household. We must return to the basics. I have often heard young parents say "I don't spank or hit my children." Well, if that is indeed the case, then that person's child does not learn to fear the repercussions of doing wrong. Later on in years, after so many years of unaddressed acting out, you have a habitual wrong doer on your hands. Then you wonder where did you go wrong. All children need structure, order, nurturing, discipline and love. The absence of any one of those things can and will prove problematic later in life. One of the problems that I see in disciplining children today is that everything is done in extremes. It seems that most people cannot, or refuse to control themselves. This is evidence of a spoiled generation. America is twisting the morals and ethics of its citizens. Many of our young people have learned to act any way they feel without any harsh penalties. We are becoming a society that is out of control. There is 'Road Rage", "Roid Rage", "Soccer-Dad Syndrome", increased suicide rates, random mass shooting and just plain maliciousness. The term "Going Postal" has become a household term. This random, uncontrolled violence is not indicative of our history. Serial killing was not our forte. We were, however, known for killing whomever it was that we were mad with. But killing everyone in the vicinity was not our thing. I personally, still do not believe that Wayne Williams was guilty of the killing of those children in Georgia in the late 1970s into the 1980s. When I learned that the "DC Snipers" were Black I was stunned. It also confirmed for me that we are definitely losing ourselves. America was founded on violence. From the Mayflower to the Indians, to the wild, wild, west; from the Civil war to the World Wars, and from Vietnam to Desert Storm, America's history is truly bloodstained. Even today, as we speak, we must ask the question, "is the war in Iraq totally necessary?" Along with their names, we are adopting their personalities and pensions for violence. Although there were many wars and conquerors in our history, our history never revealed this kind of debauchery and deviant behavior. We are the descendants of the original keepers of the planet. Our origins are of nurturing, naturally friendly people. We have historically welcomed our enemies to sit at our table. We nurtured and cared for their young. The Rev. Jesse Jackson and the late former Secretary of Commerce Ron Brown along with many others proved that our diplomacy could soften the most tyrannical dictators when others had failed miserably. Both America and Europe have forged extremely violent histories and we, as Black Americans, are assuredly adopting those violent ways. Even in the homeland, we are attempting to "Ethnically Cleanse" our own kind. The violence in Africa is horrific and can only be described as genocide and we must place the origin of this genocide in colonization.

 We, as a people, must regain our composure, re-establish our pride and do what we do best. Nurture. Our children are the victims of our metamorphosis into the American way. We should not discipline our children with anger when they do something wrong. We should discipline them with love. The mistakes they make are a major part of the learning process. I can honestly say that I did not know what my parents meant when they often said, right before beating my butt for something that I had done wrong, "This is going to hurt me more than it will you." That statement made no sense to me until I had children of my own. The incredible love that I have for them made me never want to cause them harm. However, I felt it was extremely important to teach them that there are repercussions for doing the wrong things. It may come as a spanking or a heavy reprimand or punishment. Later on it may come as jail time or the loss of something precious. But, no matter what form it may take, there will always be repercussions for doing the wrong thing. Everything that is done with true love is detectable and although, to a child it may not be known at that particular moment, the lessons will always eventually reveal themselves.

Our expectations for our children have dwindled to an alarmingly low level. On the flip side of that, some expectations exceed that which a child should have to bear. We, as parents should stop and contemplate the repercussions of our expectations on our children. Think about the stage of growth and maturity of your child and then set the standards for them. Our children are growing up too fast and the real joys of childhood are lost to them. We put too much responsibility on them when they are young and consequently, once they are free from us many of them revert back to childhood well into their thirties and forties, especially the males. A sound and happy childhood is the foundation for a well-rounded and grounded adulthood. If your child has difficulty meeting the standards that you have set for them, stop, re-evaluate the level of your child's maturity, then nurture and encourage them slowly. Try to keep your child a child during their childhood years and don't press them to grow up too fast. Under no circumstances do we discourage, dismiss or degrade our children and never give up on them.

As mentioned earlier, despite the obstacles and limitations that have been placed before our people, we have still excelled in every aspect of life. A Black doctor performed the first open heart surgery and a Black doctor discovered penicillin. Black people have invented many, many of the things that we use in everyday life like the traffic light, the ironing board, the mailbox, the computer, the record player, the helicopter and so on and so on. I have included a list of some of the things that Black people have invented.

Parents, you should teach your children of these things. If you, the parent, don't know, then you and your children should learn about them together. Go out and research and find proof in print and give them to your child to study. Help your child to be proud of his or her Blackness. Yes, there are some black history facts that they will learn in school, but there are many, many more that they will never hear about unless you instill in them an eagerness to learn more about their legacy and the power within them.

We must teach our children how to survive and at the same time teach them that uncontrolled anger and violence is not the way. The side in a battle or fight that loses control and the ability to think critically normally loses the war. Oh, he or she may win that particular battle by brute strength, but they will lose the war. For example, two young men argue over something simple. One of the young men loses his temper and loses control. In a fit of blind rage he kills the other young man. In some twisted and destructive way he has won this deadly battle. However, in the scheme of the big picture, he has lost much more than he gained. He has now taken the life of another human being, a fellow warrior. Not an enemy, but his brother. There is no returning from the destruction of any life. He has also forfeited his own life to life in prison, death by lethal injection or the electric chair (yes, some states still have the electric chair). Even if he is not caught he will spend the rest of his life running from the demons of that fateful day. It is a miserable existence. It is actually a no-win situation.

The statements made by comedian/actor Bill Cosby angered many parents. I guess there is some truth to the old saying 'the truth hurts'. Mr. Cosby's delivery may have been a bit too harsh and his placement of blame a great deal misdirected, but his subject matter was right on target. Why so many Black people took offense to his statements reveals one of two messages to me:

1. Black people don't want the truth to come out (as if it is a secret).
2. We don't even recognize the truth and its affects.

If Not Now, When?

BLACK INVENTORS AND THEIR INVENTIONS

Paper	–	*Africans*
Chess	–	*Africans*
Medicine	–	*Africans*
Urinalysis Machine	–	*Dewey Sanderson*
Horse Riding Saddle	–	*WM.D. Davis*
Postal Letter Box	–	*P.B. Downing*
Rotary Engine	–	*Andrew J. Beard*
Toilet (commode)	–	*T. Elkins*
Home Security Sys.	–	*Marie Brown*
Guitar	–	*Robert Flemming Jr.*
Ironing Board	–	*Sarah Boone*
Air Conditioning Unit	–	*Frederick M. Jones*
Printing Press	–	*W.A. Lavalette*
Internal Combustion Engine	–	*F. M. Jones*
Elevator	–	*Alexander Miles*
Telephone System	–	*Granville T. Woods*
Traffic Signal	–	*Garrett Morgan*
Roller Coaster	–	*Granville T. Woods*
Clothes Dryer	–	*G.T. Sampson*
Helicopter	–	*Paul E. Williams*
Cellular Phone	–	*Henry Sampson*
Blood Plasma	–	*Dr. Charles Drew*
Space Shuttle Retrieval Arm	–	*WM. Harwell*
Programable Remote Controls	–	*J.N. Jackson*

The Black Inventions Museum
P.O. box 76122, Los Angeles, CA, 90076

The critics of Mr. Cosby's speech say that it is counterproductive to "air our dirty laundry in public." During a conversation with Rev. Jesse Jackson at an annual Rainbow/PUSH conference Mr. Cosby responded by stating, *"Your dirty laundry gets out of school at 2:30 every day. It's cursing on the way home, on the bus, train and in the candy store. They are cursing and grabbing each other and going nowhere. And, the book bag is very, very thin because there's nothing in it."*

Number two would explain a great deal of the situations that we are faced with today. We are blind and can't see the truth! We have been so conditioned that we don't even realize that many of our own actions perpetuate our dilemma. But I don't think that is the case at all. What I see is an aimless, leaderless flock wandering around and bumping into each other. Not knowing which way to turn or where to begin to change our lives and our status here in America is a large part of the problem. The truth is that there are role models all around us everyday. There are people who have risen above the confusion and aimlessness and took action to change their station. Everyday someone somewhere springs up from the crowd and takes off on the road to some level of success. Unfortunately, most of the time this only works for that individual's benefit. Very few are inspired enough by his or her deeds to get up and follow in his or her footsteps or learn from their success. Consequently, the majority of the crowd still stumbles along aimlessly. In his book "The Mis-Education of the Negro", Dr. Carter G. Woodson said this;

> "When you control a man's thinking you do not have to worry about his actions. You do not have to tell him not to stand here or go yonder. He will find his 'proper place' and will stay in it. You do not need to send him to the back door. He will go without being told. In fact, if there is no back door, he will cut one for his special benefit. His education makes it necessary."
>
> *Dr. Carter G. Woodson, 1933*

As in any race of people, as I mention before, there are those who will rise above the lot. However, no other people has been as methodically mis-educated as our people. The masses still, to this day, suffer from the slave mentality. What Mr. Cosby neglected to take into consideration is this very fact. All peoples depend on leadership for direction and purpose. In his illustrious career, Mr. Cosby has never, until now, spoken out in defense of the Black experience and has denounced any desire to be a leader at all. He places the blame for our situation squarely on the backs of the poor and under-educated. Although the most successful endeavor of his depiction of the 'Huxtables', which I thoroughly enjoyed as a young man, was a clean, respectable and positive image of a black middle-class family, it did not relate to the troubles of the families that he so vehemently attacks. It did not serve as an example of how they should live or help them to resolve their problems.

There are many other people who quietly assume the leadership role and do so with humility and passion, however, they don't have enough resources to even attempt to purchase NBC. Many others who have achieved success feel the same way that Mr. Cosby feels. They have done their part. Well, the ghost of the infamous 'Lynch Letter' has also done its part. Many years after the fact we are still afraid to come together. We are still coming to the defense or rescue of those who are truly responsible for the mental state of our people. In our early days of freedom many ex-slaves refused to leave their masters, some refused because they thought that their masters had treated them well. Others feared the unknown and yet others feared the repercussions of the angry white mobs. Mr. Cosby has circumvented the issue and *"let the true culprits off the hook again".* (Dyson, 2005) The real issue today is not who should wear the blame; it is where do we go from here. Today, many blacks fear stepping out of their comfort zones or leaving what they know best. Poor people, who have descended from generations of poor people, oft times know nothing else and simply follow in the footsteps of their forefathers, for that is what they were taught. The same goes for people who descended from generations of educators or successful businessmen, they follow the lessons that their families have passed down. I acknowledge the exceptions in both of those scenarios. The slavery factor and the mis-education of the black man are very important to our task. It is important that we identify the origin of many of our problems so that we can address them and resolve them. That is the core of this revolution that I am referring to in this book. The renowned author, Michael Eric Dyson, in his book "Is Bill

Cosby Right (or has the black middle class lost its mind?), eloquently dissects this subject and establishes some extremely valid points. In addressing the title of Mr. Dyson's book, I don't think that the black middle-class has lost its mind, I simply think that many of those that have reached a certain level of success sincerely believe that the residual effects of slavery do not affect them. They either ignore or fail to recognize the fact that as slaves we were pitted against each other from the beginning. There was the house nigger vs. the field nigger, the light skinned nigger vs. the dark skinned nigger, they even discouraged like field niggers from associating too closely with each other. Today, we see the same scenario. The upper-middle-class blaming the lower classes for being poor and uneducated is self-destructive and self-serving. Black people of the upper and middle-class, what do you really own? Do you own successful businesses employing eager young white middle-class associates? Or do you own successful plants in the black community employing hard working black family men and women helping them to further their pursuit of the American dream?

When the revolution finally reaches full stride, many of those successful individualists who forget those left behind may have the luxury of a choice of which side they would like to be on, but, there is absolutely no doubt whatsoever, on which side they will be placed. Those who are our real enemies will automatically placed them back down with the rest of us or recruit them to infiltrate and sabotage us. Those of us who are serious about the revolution will cast them aside as our 'invisible enemy'. In this country, more than any other place in the world, we need each other to survive. We must teach our children that there is no 'me' in 'we', and there is loneliness and sadness in going down alone. We must teach our children that there was definitive intent in teaching slaves to hate one another and punish them for gathering together for anything other than working or church. The slave owners understood that there is strength in numbers; therefore, they had to divide to conquer. This strategy has lasted hundreds of years and it still works today. One of the major differences is that they don't have to lynch and murder us to keep us separate any longer; we do the job for them now. We murder each other for frivolous reasons and destroy our own neighborhoods. We rape and prostitute our own women and molest and abuse our own children. In fact, we are so much more competent at destroying ourselves than any of our enemies ever were. It seems that they taught us well. Our children are killing each other on a daily basis to what benefit even they cannot explain. Those are our young warriors and future promise out there killing themselves and we are too afraid to intervene. Well, we are not the only ones watching this genocide. Somewhere out there our true enemies are watching the same thing with a victorious grin on their faces. Please don't get it mixed up. Although reports and statistics say the membership among the Klu Klux Klan and the Arian Nation have dwindled, there are still thousands of Americans who hate us and wish us harm. Some of them are in high seats with political and religious clout and some are in positions of great wealth and power and control many of the things that we need to progress or that we need stopped or changed because it hinders our progress. We must give our children direction and help them establish constructive goals. We must teach them that in order to fight fire with fire they must gain positions of power and clout. Only then can we even consider victory. But remember to also teach the children that one person against an army of thousands is an easy target. But an army of thousands with a great leader and a just cause has the odds on their side.

The human mind is like a strange looking muscle. It needs to be exercised regularly to stay sharp and fed daily to stay healthy and active. We, as a people, are great thinkers and originators. We are the *'inventors of necessity'*. Education is a tool that can also be used as a weapon and we must teach our children to respect education and the important role that it plays in our evolution. Our schools have become breeding grounds for prospective gang members. In some instances they have become shooting galleries and death traps. We must, I repeat, we must reclaim our schools. Our children need a secure institution that is conducive to learning. We must merge and converge to create change and demand academic excellence for our children.

In the fifties and sixties, black communities were extremely poor, but they functioned as villages. Adults in those communities knew which kids belonged to which parents and everyone knew when a stranger was lurking about. Adults did not fear the children of the neighborhood because even the toughest thug showed some level of respect to the elders of that community. Yes, there was crime and plenty of criminals to commit them, but there was also a respect that permeated throughout the community.

Today, all of that has gone to the wayside and the sad fact is that no one has taken those things away from us. We, as a people, simply lost focus and gave them away. I, personally, am from the 'old school' and I cannot imagine fearing my child. If my child should disrespect me or ever threaten me or even cause me to feel threatened, then I would bring to life the old parental adage, "I brought you into this world and I will take you out!" Respect and fear of repercussion must be instilled in a child before he learns to talk and walk. In my opinion, a child should not be allowed to 'talk back' to an adult until he is old enough to reasonably and civilly express sensible grounds for such debate. There are no sensible grounds for a debate against a child being instructed to complete an assigned chore as part of the daily operations of that particular household.

Many young people today do not respect life because they have had life to this point relatively easy. They do not respect material gains because as children they receive way too many things without having to sacrifice or work for them. They do not respect their elders because many adults don't command it unequivocally. They do not respect themselves because they have not been given a reason to. What do they hear and see for the most part about themselves? Just look at Maury Povich or Jerry Springer, listen to the daily news and watch an afternoon of music videos and you will see what I mean. The reflection many teens see in the mirror is a negative image that can only see a way out through drug dealing, gang violence, entertainment or sports. Is there anyone in a child's environment that is emphasizing to any child, 'so what, if you can't sing, rap or play ball, you can always be an engineer or scientist'! We are allowing our children to fall to the wayside.

III
TEACHERS AND THE SCHOOL SYSTEM

I have heard about the diminished quality of teachers being accepted into the school systems of our communities. I have met with and talked to many of them and I have yet to meet one who was in it for the money. Many of them had a piece of their heart invested in their job. One of the problems is within the school system itself. There is so much bureaucracy and red tape involved in what they can and cannot teach that it ties their hands making it even more difficult to do their jobs. The principals have become more businessmen and women or politicians than they are educators. Lawsuits and political correctness hold priority over innovation and higher standards. Another problem facing the teachers in today's society is the parents. In an odd twist of fate the teachers and the parents have become adversaries. I have witnessed parents ready to virtually assault a teacher because the teacher spoke ill of or criticized their child.

 I read an article recently in the Atlanta Journal Constitution where a parent with a child in a Metro Atlanta school is in the process of suing the school because her son was suspended for failing to adhere to the school's dress code policy. There was a rule in the school regarding students wearing their pants in the "sag" style. The "sag" style is the wearing of pants down below the hips around the buttocks. The mother vehemently defended her son's right to dress anyway he wanted. To me, this is incredible! Since when does a child have the authority to make or break the rules? I, personally, am a staunch believer in the school uniform initiative, especially in today's society. I am not such a prude that I don't understand that each new generation has its own style. But, there is a time and place for everything. Exposed bellies, butts and thongs have no place in a classroom. School uniforms and dress codes negate the need for competition in which kid can afford the latest styles and focuses on performance and positive attitude. Each generation has also had its own slang or street language. However, years ago, that language was only allowed in the street and with your homeboys. It wasn't allowed in the home and definitely not in the classroom. Does anyone today realize that one must master his native language in order to succeed academically and/or professionally. I was amazed to discover that some of our most successful rappers like Ludacrist and Common completed high school and attended college before embarking on their musical careers.

Teachers are being cursed out, assaulted and ignored by little disrespectful adolescents who have no respect for the institution, the learning process, their elders or themselves for that matter. I acknowledge that the parents of many of these children are but children themselves. But, if you take on the responsibility of parenting a child you must also consider the well being, mental health and future of the child you are bearing. If a parent has taught his or her child to be responsible from the beginning, then, if early pregnancy should happen, being a responsible parent should not be as difficult a task as it would for some wild child who runs the street unchecked.

We are spoiling our children in following the teachings of today's child psychologists. They speak of 'time-outs' and military schools while their children are advancing swiftly into waves of suicide and mass killings and making bombs in their bedrooms. Simple things like a rule saying that teachers should not make markings in red or give out red 'F's because it makes the student feel degraded.

If Not Now, When?

Earning a failing grade is degrading! A child should feel inspired to do better or at least try harder. Most of our children simply expect the rewards afforded them without doing any work. Many of them think that a computer, DVD and CD players, large screen TV with cable and one hundred dollar sneakers automatically come with a bedroom. How is a child expected to study, achieve and create in such an amusement park environment? I remember slamming my bedroom door after an argument with my mom. When I returned from school the following day I found my room wide open and doorless. My father had removed the door from its hinges and calmly reminded me that I did not own anything in that house. The door, the room and everything else belonged to him and I will not get that door back until *He* is sure that I have learned my lesson.

Many parents send spoiled, undisciplined, disrespectful children to spend a major part of their day and the majority of each week to school and expect the teacher to raise them. Should we require parenting classes as part of the criteria for teaching degrees? I think not. Teaching a young child and holding their attention is a very important task and a hell of a job in itself. Teachers should not have to teach respect and discipline, they should motivate and educate. That is what they are paid to do. If we all did our jobs more effectively at home, maybe the teachers would be more effective at school.

The demands of living a quality life here in America are great. But one of the greatest gifts that GOD has blessed us with is a child. We should not allow our quest for nice things to override the importance of raising our children. Latchkey children is a negative term that has gained popularity in our society today. I know that it is sometimes totally unavoidable. However, parents in such situations should make extra efforts and sacrifices to rear and teach their children about the better qualities of life, like humility, patience and respect.

Our country speaks with a forked tongue when it comes to our children. One side speaks of a child's inability to consent or be responsible for his or her actions, while the other side grants adult rights and decision-making authority to these same children. Now, they are reconsidering such double talk as they are forced to give harsher penalties to the increasing numbers of undisciplined and violent young offenders. Sending these unruly children to school has created a domestic war zone and teachers should be getting hazardous duty pay. If it were up to me teachers and police officers would be making the salaries of some top executives and athletes. Teachers and Police Officers risk their lives and their sanity daily to teach our children, hold promise to our future, instill order and keep us safe.

On January 13, 2006 a program aired on 20/20 titled "Stupid In America". The program discussed the underachievement of our children in the American school system. Earlier I stated that most of the teachers I talked with had a piece of their hearts in their job. There were also some that were just collecting a paycheck and others were there for the health benefits. Unfortunately, there were some there whose mission was simply accessibility to children for their own sick and perverted reasons. Teacher's unions have helped in destroying the school system. Incompetent teachers are defended by these unions and continue to work despite their ineffectiveness in the classroom. Our students, when matched with students at the same grade level in other poorer countries come up terribly short in comparative tests. Further investigation revealed that Charter schools prove much more successful and they have no unions. In other words, teachers that don't perform up to standard are fired. The show was very informative and gave me another outlook on education here in America. The majority of our children want to learn, and they are hungry for knowledge. We, the citizens of this country are failing our children. We have the responsibility of protecting our children's best interest. If we are not aware of the failings of our school system, how do we correct them? If we do not participate in the education of our children, how does this situation improve? As parents we must police the politics of our own communities and demand, not request, demand change for the better. We cannot wait for the government to make a change in our communities. We must act and act now. Our black brothers and sisters with political clout and financial advantages must come together and create better educational institutions for our children. We must reach them with studies that relate to their life's experiences and teach them how to improve their stations with lessons that address those matters that have been historically lacking in this present state of education. Other peoples have done just that. In the book, 'The Mis-Education of The Negro', the esteemed Dr. Carter G. Woodson addresses this fact. Of our antiquated school system, he states,

> *"In history, or course, the Negro had no place in this curriculum. He was pictured as a human being of the lower order, unable to subject passion to reason, and therefore useful only when made the hewer of wood and the drawer of water for others. No thought was given to the history of Africa except so far as it had been a field of exploitation for the Caucasian."*
>
> *(Woodson, 1933)*

As do others, we must teach our own if we ever expect to supply them with the proper education that would benefit them the most.

Some years ago, an incident occurred at the middle school that my twin daughters attended. A gang of female students beat up another young female student. The next day, the victim entered the school with a large butcher knife and began to attack any student that she thought was involved in her beating. Several children were injured. A town meeting was called at the school for parents, community leaders and Board of Education members. I was furious and there was no way that I would miss this meeting. More than I was furious, I was disheartened to see that there were more Board members on stage than there were parents in the audience. This is indicative of our participation in the education of our children. Yes, there were some very concerned parents in attendance besides myself, and we were all outraged. But there were not enough there to make a difference. The parent of the child who was attacked was not even there.

Although it is not expressed nearly enough, children are our most precious commodity. They hold the future of the human race in their little hands. They are the future doctors and scientists who will discover the cures for AIDS and cancer. They are the inventors who will discover an alternate means of obtaining energy without destroying the planet. They are the future politicians who will pursue world peace and prepare the world for their own offspring. If we continue to let them down then they will fail in their task and the world, as we know it, will end. For the mothers, fathers and teachers who are trying to achieve excellence in parenting and teaching, I applaud you. For those of you who are not, I implore you. No child asked to be here, but each and every one of them are gifts from GOD. If you partake in the ritual of acceptance for one of these gifts, then you accept the responsibility that comes along with it. There is no greater pride than raising a child and teaching him the right way and having him or her grow into a successful, GOD fearing and contributing adult. His or her contributions may save the world.

IV
BLACK MEN!

Oh, my twisted and deceived brothers. We have abandoned our mission and the importance of our place in the success of our village. We have been totally disillusioned as to what being a real man really means. Being a real man has nothing at all to do with how many women you have conquered or how many cars you have. It has nothing to do with how much money or bling you have either. A man with millions is no more man than the one living from paycheck to paycheck. The state of real manhood is much, much simpler than that. In considering the true nature of man, there are really only four rules to fulfilling that title.

1. The ability to procreate, nurture and provide for your tribe.
2. The ability and willingness to protect your tribe against all who encroach or threaten your village.
3. The ability to adapt to and rule any environment that you are confronted with.
4. The ability to teach the young children of your village, both male and female what a real man is supposed to do.

Let us take a moment to review, in detail, these simple rules individually.

Rule #1: To procreate (reproduce) – To assist in perpetuating the human race; to participate in the process of fertilization for the purpose of creating new life.

This does not mean wandering all over your village randomly impregnating as many women as possible. On the contrary, it means responsibly fathering offspring that you can afford. By using the term afford I mean being able to execute the necessary responsibilities of fatherhood. These responsibilities include the providing of food and shelter, nurturing, teaching, protecting and disciplining. To the young brothers: How many of you are trying to do all of the things mentioned above? In my research I have found that the number of those who are trying far out-weigh the number of those who don't. The problem lies in the fact that the public rarely hears of those who do try while the court system here in America makes it hard to fulfill those responsibilities and survive at the same time for those who don't live in the same household as their children. Some men actually feel that it is not their responsibility to raise the children that they father. Whether that is a form of denial or a symptom of poisoned upbringing is a moot question. What do we do and when does the cycle end, is the important question.

We are blessed with the ability to participate in the process of creating new life not to bolster our libido and show what kind of stud or player we are, but very simply for the propagation of the human race; in other words, to keep the race going on into the future. The children are our future and if we (men) don't teach them to become good men and women then they will learn from other less savory sources, like television. A child having free rein in his/her accessibility to the television set is like sending a child to idiot camp. The television has in fact become an adversary to the art of parenting.

The act of having intercourse (sex) with the opposite sex is indeed a pleasurable act, and it can even be a great deal of fun. However, if not done responsibly, it can devastate a young life (especially females), and now, in too many cases, it can kill. Teaching abstinence is a wasted task. I remember when my hormones were raging and there was nothing anyone could possibly say to deter me from exploring my sexuality. Teaching responsibility is much more important. Also inspiring a child to set high goals and teaching them to work hard for anything that they want teaches them responsibility and appreciation for all of the rewards that will come their way. I believe that if you teach children to be responsible then they will make better decisions concerning their lives.

Men, one of the greatest responsibilities of a man is to provide sustenance, shelter and security to his family. We, as men, must get our priorities straight. There is only one bottom line. Survival. It is our duty to ensure that our tribe has everything it needs to survive. Everything else is secondary. Once you have provided all of the needs, then you can concentrate on the wants. To be a real man you must work hard and be willing to sacrifice. Many men are under the impression that only women need to sacrifice. In order to be a wife and mother women must sacrifice their dreams, goals, many of their wants and sometimes their health and meals to ensure that the family gets what they need. Men cannot sacrifice those things because his relentless pursuit of his dreams, goals, wants and health all revolve around making a better home for his family. Such garbage. Real men take care of their wives as well as their children. As the wife is always the backbone and foundation of the family, her man should be prepared to do whatever is necessary to ensure her needs are fulfilled.

The nurturing that men provide for the children is different from the nurturing from women. Men should nurture by providing a sense of security for all of the children of their village, not just their own. Men should provide examples of stability, integrity and honesty. Men should teach young boys to be good men, work hard and be responsible. They should teach them how to treat and respect their mother and all other women in their lives. They should teach young boys how to work and how to take care of themselves. They should also teach young girls what a good man looks like.

I mentioned earlier about it being the responsibility of real men to provide food and shelter. Often in today's society the woman makes more money than the man. This occurrence should not disturb the natural order of things. The man should still provide security and stability and should also work hard to bring home whatever he can.

This is also not to say that men should not participate in the other responsibilities of running a household, like cooking, cleaning and rearing the children; especially if the woman works hard to contribute in other ways.

> Rule #2. The ability and willingness to protect your tribe against all who encroach upon or threaten your village.

We as men spend too much time battling ourselves. We fight against our brothers, we attack our sisters and we abuse our children, neither of which is our enemy. Our true enemy is anyone who attacks our family or who attempts to deprive our tribe of anything it needs to survive. Many of us cower from our enemies, or if we do attack, it is with mindless abandon. True warriors master the art of war and attack with strategy. We as men and warriors must be willing to die to protect our tribe and village and the village should be prepared to care for our loved ones should death occur during a valiant battle against the enemies of our tribe and village. Recent history has shown our people, especially our men, rebelling against our enemies by destroying our own communities. We brutishly and mindlessly burn our own villages to the ground. Our tribe then suffers from our actions. Men of every village should come together respectively and create a strategy to protect our villages from any enemy that threatens our quality of life. An example of what I am talking can be seen in the movie "The Deacons for Defense". No matter what your station in life, there should always be a quality of life worth protecting.

I have lived in several communities, from the lower to the middle class, where a crime watch has been created and the majority of volunteers have always been women. Men, real men, where are you!!

> Rule #3: The ability to adapt to and rule any environment that you are confronted with.

Sometimes we are dealt a truly bad hand. Hurricane Katrina is a prime example of such an occurrence. Without warning and with a sudden violence that only Mother Nature can wield, everything that we owned is destroyed. We are left homeless and destitute. Men, it is your responsibility to take whatever hand you are dealt and play it to your best ability. It will, no doubt, take time to rebuild and regain all of the things that you have lost and there are some loses that can never be recaptured, however, the day after is when you begin to adapt. As long as your health permits, you should start playing your hand and not let your hand play you. I know that this may sound too damned simple. But the simple fact is that it is that damned simple. There are examples of the success stories occurring everyday. Although it has only been some months since that horrible disaster, many men have gotten their families back to some semblance of normal life, even if they had to totally relocate. Men, women in love are very strong. A black women who has her family as her number one priority will back her man to the ends of the earth as long as he proves himself worthy.

I have searched websites and newspapers and found many job opportunities for laborers and professionals. Many people from out of the state are applying for these jobs because, in some instances, the pay is pretty good. Many of these contractors are jumping on the opportunity to get large government contracts for the rebuilding process and some just plain want to help. Whatever the reason, it is all an opportunity to re-establish security for your tribe. For the rest of us who have never experienced so great a tragedy, what excuse should we have? Life and times get extremely frustrating, but there is never a reason to give up. Especially when your tribe needs you. As I mentioned earlier, a good woman appreciates a man who, no matter what the odds, gets up everyday and gives his best to provide for his family. If you cannot find regular work then go out and barter your services for food or shelter. Please don't sit and wait for the government or anyone else to grant you a handout. All help is appreciated, but the sooner you, as a man, gets out there and gets on his feet, the sooner and closer your tribe gets back to some quality of life. There is no obstacle outside of death that a Black man can't overcome. If you are angry or depressed, turn it into positive energy and work with a vengeance. If you are sad because of the state of your family, then bringing what your family needs home will make you feel better. Overcoming all obstacles and being the provider is what you were born to do. If your woman finds a job first or finds a better job, then the men must continue to make that household the best home and the safest home it could possibly be.

Rule #4: The ability to teach the young children of your village, both male and female what a real man is suppose to do.

My brothers, your entire life will serve as a teaching tool. As a child you taught your parents how to handle the trials and tribulations that a child in the new generation is faced with. You taught your teachers how to adjust their strategies to hold your attention. As an adult several people will scrutinize your actions; your boss is watching you to see if you are worthy of promotion; your wife is watching and learning how to please you and keep you healthy and motivated. Your daughter looks to you for security and lessons on what kind of man she should marry. Your son looks to you to teach him how to be a man and your village should look to you for your wisdom, protection and the security that you should be providing.

Just think that if we had a village full of real men who fulfilled these four simple rules or principles, how strong, safe and progressive that village would be!

During my tenure working with prison inmates I held impromptu counseling sessions with them. During one particular session, I presented a question to about thirty young men. The question was, "Are you a man, and if so, what makes you a man?"

The replies that I received from these incarcerated young men; white, black and Hispanic alike, were depressing. One young brother jumped to his feet and defiantly stated, "Yo man, I am All Man. Ain't no punk in me!" The others chimed in behind him, "Word!" I continued on with the second part of the question. "What makes you a man?" The first young man replied with, "Ah'm rollin' with 'ten inches' and Ah got 'ho's in every area code' *and* six kids." Another brother shouted out, "Ah do what I gotta do to survive and Ah ain't scared of nothin' and nobody!" I asked the second brother, "Do you have any children?" His reply was simply, "Yeah." A young white man stood up and said, "Ah got a family at home and a job; Ah jus' got caught out there." I asked, "Do you realize that putting yourself out there to get caught has jeopardized the welfare and future of all that you have created; their safety and welfare is one of the main responsibilities of being a real man?" "Think about it; a man is suppose to be able to take care of himself and his tribe. You, every last one of you, are being told when to wake up in the morning, when to eat; you are being fed, housed and told what to do and then told when to go to bed. You are supplying your families with nothing; you are producing nothing and you are going nowhere. When you leave here, your status will be exactly the same as it was when you got here. The only thing that can possibly change is your attitude about what being a real man really is. You will have lost time, but not promise."

Black men in this country as a whole have always been self-destructive and individualistic. We must realize that the state that we exist in today was indeed a plan. If you don't know of the speech given on the banks of the James River in 1712 by William Lynch to the slave owners regarding the ways and means of controlling their slaves, you should take a moment to look it up and study it. There have been arguments contending that the letter was actually a hoax, however, the continuity, especially in the south, in which the slave owners all practiced the same tactics and the end result of such treatment lends itself to some truth to the contents of the letter. Look around you and even look at yourselves in many cases. You will find that the lasting effects of slavery are still being passed down from generation to generation. It is time for us to grab the reins and steer our people away from this vicious cycle. It is the responsibility of Black men to repair the damage and start to rebuild and renew. The time for acting like crabs in a barrel must end now. Instead of pulling one another down, we must support and respect one another. Just look in any state, especially in states with large urban communities. We are the only people in the whole United States that don't run our own communities. The Italians have a "Little Italy" everywhere that there is a concentration of them, as do the Jewish people and the people from the Middle East. The Chinese people have "China Towns" and the people of Latin or Hispanic persuasion have their own communities. These areas are always identifiable because once you enter into them, if you don't speak the language, you can't read the signs. They own the businesses and keep their customs and cultures in their communities.

Black men born from generations here in America lack the ability to work together and/or gather together constructively for a single cause unless it is church; and that only last through Sunday. We don't run businesses in our community. We even have limited control of the politics in our community. The Taiwanese, Koreans, and Vietnamese run the grocery and clothing stores, the Jewish businessmen run the jewelry and furniture stores and the Italians run the liquor stores. Sure, this is an exaggeration, but too much of it is true. I know that there are some very progressive Black men in just about every community who own businesses and property. The problem is that there is not enough of them to make a difference. Most of the big business conducted in our communities is conducted by White America. Where does that leave us? It should leave us in a state of rebellion. Now is the time. Those above the middle class are getting richer and those below it are getting poorer. I am mad and ready to do something about it. What about you, my brothers?

Black men, it is time to stop thinking of and treating our women like bitches. Even worst, we call them bitches as if it is a GOD-given name. We have assisted in the degradation of our women to the extent that they call themselves bitches as a term of endearment. Negative words have little meaning to me, however, this particular practice leaves the door open for others to degrade our women and treat them the same way. It also forces our sisters who will not stand for such disrespect to look elsewhere for better treatment. We desperately need to learn to respect each other, especially our women. We need them to survive.

Our fear of true commitment must also be eradicated. The black family has always been the backbone of our race. We may not have wealth and property to pass down through the generations, but we have always had family pride, integrity and traditions to pass down. This we are losing. The average black family has become a mother and her children. The warriors have gone astray. We live in a disposable generation. Everything is disposable. If it is not disposable, it is microwaveable. Quick, easy and when you are done, you simply throw it away. This is how many of us live our lives. We search high and low for the 'quick and easy' or the 'hook up'. Most things obtained through the 'quick and easy' are not appreciated as much as some things that are worked for. Come on, my brothers, do you want the woman that you met in the club last night and had sex with in your car that same night to be your girlfriend or wife? Even marriage is disposable today. Many people get married for the wrong reason. They then find that the reason they got married in the first place is not worth living in misery with someone they can't

If Not Now, When?

stand. Then there is the lack of commitment to the commitment that we have made. After we have settled in and life becomes routine, we get bored because the thrill is now gone. So we venture out into the world searching for some excitement. Maybe it's the fact that the fine young philly that you fell in love with has gained some weight and no longer has all the time she once had before the babies and the house to take care of herself. Whatever the excuse, the thrill is now gone. Brothers, grow up. Marriage is not about the thrill. It is about real life. It is about gaining stability and security. It is about creating a family unit for support, both spiritually and emotionally, till death do us part. That is why we get married in the eyes of GOD. It is about finding that one person that you can trust and truly show yourself. I can speak of these things boldly because I too have played victim to the self-destruction that is so familiar to the Black man. Even today, I fight daily to fend off such destructive behavior and sometimes I lose the battle for the day. But, the war goes on in my heart and I will continue to fight everyday.

We have become reckless. Too easily we give in to the desires of the flesh. We are destroying the fabric of our existence. The Black Family. The unity and support of the black family is what helped us survive all of those years of slavery and discrimination. Our greatest leaders were members of supportive families. As quiet as it is kept, those women were just as great as those men because they suffered for the cause too. They also gave the ultimate sacrifice; the men that they loved and the head of their families.

Now, tell me, educate me, and convince me that this is all right. What is up with this 'down-low' thing? I truly believe that some people are born with feminine tendencies, hormonal imbalances and even female brain activity in a man's body. But if you have lived as a man, assumed the duties of a man, offered love and security to a woman and created a family as a man should, then why do you give in to these sinful atrocities. (Understand my position. To a homosexual personality, same sex encounters are natural and normal, but to a heterosexual personality, these things are atrocities). One of the reasons is that there is no restraint in the world anymore. As I have said before, people can either no longer control themselves or they simply refuse to control themselves. There is no longer a commitment to the word of GOD or a commitment to manhood or a commitment to family and love. There seems to be only a commitment to money and the desires of the flesh. The fact that you vowed under the eyes of GOD to honor your wife through sickness and health, until death do you part and then you have sex with another man, confirms it for me. I am proud of being a Black Man, my father taught me how to be a proud Black Man and I am committed to that fact. Why have we become so weak to the desires of the flesh?

Black men, especially, must think twice before consenting to such destructive weaknesses. From the age of 0 to 20 years of age, we lived for ourselves. It was all about us back then. All that was important was what we received from others. After the age of 20 we are no longer considered a boy. We are now accountable for our actions and the responsibilities of a man begin to befall us. We should now be thinking of our future. Eventually, the responsibilities include a family. We are no longer living for ourselves. Our purpose in life now takes on a more universal meaning. Our younger generation is living the life of a child, well into their thirties and forties. Living jobless, without any direction, with your pants down around your hips, and with your parents are not the signs of manhood. Making babies that you can't take care of and standing on some corner all day getting high with the rest of your boys is just that; acting like boys; irresponsible teens with not a care in the world. Could this be why so many of our women are so lonely and desperate? Could this be why so many of them cling to some thug flinging money around so that they can say they got something out of the deal? Our women have very slim pickings with so many of our men in prison, on drugs, destitute, lost or gay. As men, our commitments develop into something more important than ourselves. Understand that whether you are married or not or have children or not, you are an icon for your people. You don't have to be a leader of your people. You, as a Black man, are a representative for your people. Outsiders will look at you and form judgments about your people. This is important because we are far from being an independent race and we need to be viewed as a proud, hardworking people with integrity. More important, our young people will look to you for lessons on how to be a Black man. So, my brother, be proud of being a Black Man. Walk the walk, talk the talk and be true to your purpose. The students of your life will someday rule the world.

V
MY BELOVED SISTERS

My misinformed and mislead sisters, you have been used throughout our history here in America. The oppressors used you as foot warmers and sex slaves. They used you to clean their homes and care for their children. They have always kept you close to their vest because they know that you are the key to our strength. They used you in their plan to destroy the black family. As described in the 'Lynch Letter' in 1712 on the banks of the James River, William Lynch stated that in order to control the slaves the slave owners must take the strongest and most willful Negro, display him in front all of the other slaves, tar and feather him, tie him to horses and set him on fire, then whip the horses and literally pull him apart. This act taught two distinct lessons to the black women. One lesson was to be independent of the black man because he can be taken away at any given moment. The second lesson was that black women should teach their daughters the same thing and worst yet, teach their sons to be subservient and careful not to cross the masters because they will kill him. The black woman was not wrong, she was responding to the conditions that she was faced with. She was only protecting her loved ones. In the 1960's they offered you assistance during hard times as long as we (Black men) didn't live with you even though there were no jobs for any of us. Even today they search you out and 'headhunt' you for high paying positions and turn away many qualified Black men in your favor. Please don't get me wrong. I am not saying that you are not qualified nor I am diminishing the progression of Black women. What I am saying is that this trend is diminishing the traditional role of the black household. What I am saying is that along with the twisted and confusing definition of manhood here in America that this trend is very hard for the Black man's already injured ego to digest. Together we must continue to nurture this progression and simultaneously repair the damaged ego of the Black man by lifting him up and helping him to stand on his own feet.

With that said, I am in no way posturing myself in the way of the progression of Black women; I simply love my Black sisters and applaud your progress. My mother is the greatest woman that I have ever known and I simply adore her. She is strong and wise; she is loving and supportive. She is the backbone of my family and has always been. She was unwaivered in her love and support of my father, who was a good man, through good and bad times. She stuck with her three sons through untimely deaths, drug use and jail sentences and she is a sterling example for her daughter. She is undoubtedly my hero. So I could never denounce the power and abilities of Black women. However, as I do Black men, I question some of the motives and goals of my precious sisters. Your role in the village is just as important as that of the brothers. We (Black men) need your support, love and strength to carry on the good fight. I know that we sometimes fight what is good for us in favor of what is good to us. I speak about our destructive ways and I call out my brothers on our faults and failures. Now it is time for me to address my sisters. As mentioned several times throughout this book, the Black man has been on a path to self-destruction for many, many years and one of the really cold hard truths is that you, my Black woman, have been an indirect and unconscious contributor to the negative tailspin that the Black man is experiencing here in America. Please do not take this personally if the shoe does not fit. But, in too many cases it does. There has always been great sisters leading the battle and there are many on the front line today.

If Not Now, When?

As we have progressed in this American society we have grown further and further apart in our goals. Again, we are all becoming more and more individualistic. When our people were first brought here on the slave ships from Africa there was only one unified goal. That goal was survival. Without each other we all would have failed; but here we are. As we have become exposed more and more to this capitalistic society, we have drifted further and further away from the ways of our homeland. This was exacerbated by the treatment of the slave owners and their goal of stripping us of all we knew. At the end of slavery our people set out in search of the basic necessities for survival; shelter, food and work. The promise of forty acres and a mule was a lie. Our people started their freedom with nothing. Black men sought to support and house their families. Jim Crow made our quest extremely difficult especially in the south, but still we made great gains. Because we had been deprived of so much, our mission was to become equal with white society and obtain what the masters had. Black men had the will and the want to provide their families with the better things in life, but the resources were difficult to find. However, despite the great odds, many flourishing black communities were formed. In many different regions throughout the United States progressive black communities like Greenwood, OK and Rosewood, Fl sprung up. In places like Chicago, Washington DC, Detroit, New York and in California towns grew into substantial communities with as many as ten thousand black citizens. The fear of the rapidly growing success of these places gave the enemies of the Black man just cause to destroy the progression of these communities. During the 1920s riots involving white mobs burning these communities to the ground occurred all over the country. Again we were left with nothing. However, the Black family survived. After the introduction of welfare in the 1960s, the beginning of the women's movement in the 1970s provided another obstacle for our people. Women began to think more individualistically. The Black man was then, and still is, too weak to battle against these obstacles. More and more Black women began to put careers in front of family. Black women began to feel that they didn't need a man to be happy. At that point, another devastating blow was given to the black family. With the Black man lost and leaderless and the Black woman's 'new-found' independence, the Black family was bound for destruction.

Many of my sisters have also lost sight of the universal goal. They also have learned to live in this disposable society. Many Black women chase and demand the materialism and capitalism of American life. For many years Black women had chased and longed for the European body type. They have straightened their hair so that it would swing and flow just like white women's hair. Even today, in the 21st century, the most popular style is super straight, jet-black hair hanging down around the shoulders. They have dieted aggressively in effort to shrink their behinds and obtain the skinny, svelte figure that they saw on television and in magazines. Many Black women yearn for the life of luxury. Fancy cars, expensive clothes and prestige now outweigh the pursuit of the security of raising a proud Black family and being part of a strong black community. If they cannot get those things from a Black man, then they will try by whatever means are necessary; some even long for maids and nannies. My beloved sisters, no one can raise a child like a Black woman. No one can nurture a family like a Black woman. Why do you think that there were so many mammies raising the children of the slave owners. The slave owners knew that they could trust you with their family; they knew that nurturing is your nature.

Over the last decade the standard of beauty all over the world has changed. Women of color in all of their glory have advanced as the icons of the world of beauty. Women everywhere want to be thicker, gain the curves that only hips and butt can provide. They are now administering collagen to their lips in effort to obtain that voluptuous look of women of color. Women everywhere are risking their lives in effort to be tanned all year round. I can actually say that I don't know if this is a blessing or a curse. Other races have always pursued women of color, but now they are becoming a commodity. This puts added pressure on the Black man who was handicapped from the beginning. Black men have to strive harder to make up ground and money to attract our own materialistic sisters.

I know that many Black men who have elevated themselves have pursued white women as a reward or trophy, one might say. I, personally, don't condone this. But in the same token, I have seen many Black women turn their nose up at a brother who has a blue-collar job and a regular car. The attraction of the 'bad boy' image is destructive to the fiber of the black family. Many of today's Black women are attracted to the 'rebel without a cause', or the brother that takes destructive risks to gain a dollar; the brother that engages in destructive activity; the brother that will slap you in the mouth, call you a bitch and subject you to all kinds of 'baby-mama-drama, then buy you something expensive. Brothers will go to many, many extremes to impress a Black woman. Many end up resorting to crime.

I am in no way blaming the Black woman for the plight of the Black man today or any other period in our history here. I am simply stating the facts that are evident. If we as a people could only see the forest for the trees, we would recognize that the William Lynch letter is still hard at work down below the surface. If only we could dream of strong, safe and secure black communities with excellent school systems and our own businesses instead of six million dollar, gated mansions with more rooms than we have relatives, or one hundred and fifty thousand dollar cars with 22's and spinners, then, maybe we could be proud of who we are and where we came from.

Raising proud black children is no longer the priority, making money is. Now, I know that money is what makes this country go and I know that we must have money to survive, however, having money as an individual and having money as a people are two different things. Having money as a people gives power to the mass. The constructive use of that power puts that people in position to challenge the powers of the ruling class. Let's look at the Jewish community as an example. They own businesses and corporations that support their own communities. They run their own schools and their own politics and practice, undaunted, their own religion. We already have the power of the largest consumer in the nation, but we eagerly give that power away while making the powers-that-be more powerful. What really would happen if we could keep that power in our own communities? Black women, you now have just as much, if not more money and power than most Black men, you are successful doctors, lawyers, power executives, entrepreneurs, politicians and business owners, where do we go from here?

We are swiftly becoming the minority among the minorities. The Latino and Hispanic communities are growing steadily as are the Korean and Vietnamese communities. Black women, you are not the blame for our predicament, but you do hold the key to our survival. We need you to challenge Black men! Most of the things we do, we do for you and your attention. Single sisters, show your power! If a married man approaches you, declare your independence and strength and tell him that you refuse to share. Tell him that his actions are destroying the Black family, therefore weakening the Black community. Tell him to go home to his wife and make some more strong Black boys so that your future daughters will not have such a rough time finding a good man.

    I truly feel for my sisters because we Black men have been acting like fools. We are either so downtrodden and beaten up that we have surrendered and given up, or we are so driven that we become selfish and egotistical. But there are some brothers who have neither given up nor have they forgotten what is important. Most of those brothers are not driving Porsches or Lamborghini's, they are driving pick up trucks or Fords and old Volvos. They are out there, they are just not exciting enough or blinging enough to be seen in the street or club. They are working hard and looking for a good woman. I know that they are scarce, but they are out there. Some of them have been beaten down by gold diggers and have resorted to playing 'the game' like everyone else, but believe me; the love of the right woman can bring him right back to his senses.

    Remember this; It's like the marketplace. It's all about supply and demand. If there is a continued demand for the thugged-out brother then the supply will continue to grow. When women begin to accept no less than the progressive, hard working, GOD fearing, conscious Black man, he will begin to change. Coming from a brother from the hood, if the thug life got a brother 'no play' at all, there would be much less thug-ism in the world today. You must see, it is all about you. If beautiful young sisters would stop flocking to auditions for videos that require them to dress scantily and dance promiscuously in the face of some thugged-out brother with gold teeth in his mouth, then eventually the thrill of the thug would peter-out, especially after the age of thirty. Isn't it amazing how many brothers hold on to the thug-life well into their thirties and forties. Well, as long as the pretty young sisters are sweating the thug-life and willing to go to the extremes to be a part of it, then the brothers will be thrilled to oblige. It's simple 'supply and demand'.

If Not Now, When?

Married sisters!! You must demand total commitment if there is to be any commitment at all. Take no shorts and leave no prisoners. If a brother wants to sleep around when he has a loving wife and kids at home, then let him sleep somewhere else permanently. Do not, I repeat, do not risk your life or the welfare of your children. Today, one cannot tell if a brother is on the down-low unless he is caught red-handed or he confesses. If he is willing to consistently cheat and sneak, then he is putting your life at risk. A brother who truly loves his woman and his family would think twice if he thought he would definitely lose them forever by engaging in such destructive behavior. Additionally speaking, it is hard out here on a brother on his own with child support payments and/or alimony, in other words, 'it's cheaper to keep her'.

We must all step up to the plate and get our priorities straight. I have seen first hand what love can do to the strongest person. We must remain strong for the sake of love. Not just for the love ourselves and our mates, but for the love of our people. My sisters, as I have stated before, you are the heart and soul of our existence. Without you the Black man is nothing. I challenge you to challenge all Black men. I challenge you to demand respect from all Black men. If all he wants is sex, then you should withhold it from him. Do not give in to being used as an object for his amusement as if he is some big kid with a toy. Your body is a temple and all Black men should worship at the altar of your essence. In order to teach men how to respect your body, you must respect it first. We already know that you know how to make it look good on the outside. But, how well do you take care of the inside. The essence of who you are is more important than what you look like on the outside. There is nothing more beautiful than the smooth, well taken care of, skin of a Black woman. This is all the more true when her essence is also well taken care of and shining through.

> *"With head held high and the glow of a thousand Black Queens Emitting from every proud sweep of your glorious hips, You are all true royalty."*
>
> *Linwood Hancock 2005*

Every Black man may not be able to shower you with gold and trinkets, but he must shower you with all of the love, honor and respect that you deserve. Accept no less, demand no more. The wealth you seek is embedded deep within Black Love. The love of yourself, the love of your family and the love of your people will fill your heart till it runneth over. I once heard an old woman say, "If you search for someone to buy you things, you will find an owner. If you search for a friend, you will find true love."

It is not a sin to want the finer things in life, but that should not be your only priority. Knowledge of who you really are, your mission in the universe and pride in your essence and in your ancestry and acknowledging that who they were and what they went through makes you who you are today, is more important. Living with that knowledge and pride will bring all the riches of royalty to you. So, my sisters, read up on yourselves. Study the history of the Black woman throughout world history. You will find that some of the greatest rulers and heroes in the world were women of color.

Do your own research:
Tiye, Nubian Queen of Egypt
Nefertari, Nubian Queen
Makeda, Queen of Sheba
Cleopatra VII, Queen of Egypt
Nandi, Queen of Zululand
Nzingha, Amazon Queen of Matamba
Hatshepsut, Queen of Far Antiquity (Egypt)
Amina, Queen of Zaria

And so on, and so on, and so on......

Raising Black children:

Raising a Black child here in America is a situation that wields a double-edged blade. If you are raising a boy, you must prepare him to face the obstacles facing young Black men in the new millennium. Things like peer pressure, gang violence, drugs, sex and other vices are a constant danger to them. Covert prejudice and hidden discrimination still prevail in this country and we must all train our children to overcome.

I have worked with prison inmates for many years and the percentage of young Black men from solid middle class homes and

If Not Now, When?

good families that have ended up in the prison system is astounding. Most of them had fallen victim to the dangers listed above. Many Black fathers are failing to fully participate in the raising of many of them and Black mothers are providing credence to that old adage "Mothers raise their daughters, but they love their sons". I have found too much truth to that saying as I have seen so many young Black men who don't know how to take care of themselves. Cleaning, cooking, ironing, budgeting and generally living with some kind of order in their lives that they have orchestrated was a rarity amongst these young men. Black mothers, while you are raising your daughters, please stop and raise your sons also. Teach them the basic skills that will help them to be independent. I find that in talking to young Black men, both in and out of prison, revealed that men raised with a solid sense of responsibility are more likely to live a more responsible life than those without such. This does not, however, guarantee that they won't get caught up in the system, but it places the odds in a positive favor on their side. In a perfect situation where the family unit is intact with responsible, conscious parents, the father teaches the son how to be a good man and the mother teaches the son how to be a good human being.

Times have changed drastically from the fifties and sixties when I grew up. Today, the dangers that face young boys are the same dangers that face our daughters. Back then, the biggest dangers were getting pregnant, getting raped or getting involved with the wrong boy (which could consequently result in the other two dangers). Today, young girls face drug addiction, gang violence, promiscuous sex, AIDS and other dangers just like the boys. Terms like 'friends with benefits' and the insane belief that oral sex is not intercourse, endanger our children daily. Years ago, when we said that we were going partying, that is just what we meant. We were going either to some specific place or even multiple places to hear some loud music, dance until we sweat and drink some wine or beer or even smoke some weed. Today, partying could mean anything from wild sex orgies to gang rape to gang banging or gang violence. Blatant promiscuity and open sex is at an apex. Even with the threat of AIDS looming overhead every single day! Acting like a young lady has literally dropped from the vocabulary in many settings. Young girls are rough and tumble, foul mouthed, sexually uninhibited and ready to mix-it-up with anyone who crosses their paths. It has always been extremely unnerving for me to see young women in the prison system. The prison system can turn even the most feminine young sister into a hardened violent mirrored image of her former self. Many young sisters dress like thugs, talk like thugs and act like thugs. In too many cases they suffer the same fate as thugs; drug addiction, gang activity, prison and violent deaths.

Earlier I mentioned the "down-low' phenomenon that has been plaguing our Black men. Homosexuality is also running rampant amongst our young women too! As I stated earlier in the section to Black men, I know that some people are born with homosexual attributes. I don't believe that there is a cure or corrective measure that can stop such an occurrence. However, I also believe that in some cases there is simply a conscious choice made to practice homosexual acts. This is wrong! It defeats our purpose in the universe. It defies the natural course of human nature. If you believe in GOD, then it is a sin against His word. If you are an atheist, then you are going against the natural evolution of man. Either way, it is wrong. The progression of this nihilist capitalistic society has steadily deteriorated the moral and ethical fiber of our people. There is no longer a thing called discretion. We have devolved into a 'no-holds-barred' existence, and we are paying for it dearly.

Although industrialization seems to be a natural part of the evolution of human beings, it is also the curse of human beings. As our minds develop and we become (ideally) smarter, we also become more destructive towards the natural flow of the universe. Industrialization is rapidly devouring our planet's natural resources and the many experiments with chemicals and pesticides are literally making people crazy. The stress level in this society is skyrocketing and so are the rates of heart attack, the stroke rate and suicide rates.

Women, you ask, "and what has this got to do with me when men run the world?" This is an understandable question. The answer is, yes, it is true that men run the world, but you run the men. Although most men would not concede to this, we would do just about anything for that thing that you alone possess. Your womanhood is your greatest weapon, yet you give it away so easily. Take hold of your assets and learn to use them for the good of mankind. Collectively, only you can bring man back to a sense of humanity. Only you have a spiritual and emotional connection with mankind within you. Inside you is where humanity is borne.

I know that I am an idealist and I dream constantly of a just, fair and humane world. I am also just sane enough to know that is a virtual impossibility. But just think that if each individual person on this planet began to truly take responsibility for his or her actions and acted in accordance with the flow of the universe, how much more harmonic life could be for all of us. From a more subjective viewpoint, if Black people here in America and all over the world could only realize their worth as a race of people, how much more good we could do in the world. Just think, if we could conceivably have done all the good that we have done as a subjugated people, how much more could we have, or can we do as a truly free people.

VI.
Men and women of the Cloth

I know that many people of both sexes and many races will be insulted by what I am about to say. This is my own opinion based on my experiences, observances and my own research.

I challenge all Black ministers, preachers, bishops, doctors and any other titles that you have been ordained into to teach the truth. The religion that has been taught to our people is a religion that was introduced to our people as a method of control. Missionaries, who, after many lost battles in attempt to overtake our warriors, were sent to Africa to colonize and take away the control of the motherland, and they initially introduced it to our people. Africans already knew of the existence of Jesus Christ. In the teachings of the Europeans, they introduced the Son of GOD as being in their image and not ours. It was of no consequence that the image that they introduced was in complete contradiction to the description of Jesus Christ in the bible.

Even the bible itself has been rewritten several times by the ruling class. At no time has any of these rewrites been conducted by Black people or any people of color. I was raised as a Baptist and attended Sunday school every Sunday until I was old enough to question my participation in this practice. At a very young age I was exposed to other religions and I began to question what I was being taught. My parents made sure that I was introduced to the "Word of GOD", and I accept the fact that more of my sense of right and wrong came from those origins. In other words, my belief in GOD, as taught in the Baptist religion has made me who I am today. But, in the same token, my search for truth in all aspects of my existence has caused me to question those teachings.

One of the first questions that I had as a young boy came when I first read the bible's description of Jesus Christ while I fanned myself with a picture of Jesus Christ that totally contradicted the description in the Bible. Every fan, every book, every crucifix, every depiction everywhere I looked bared this image of complete contradiction. Yet, no one seemed to question it. It was never presented as a sermon in any church that I had visited. It was never an issue.

How important would it be for a people to worship a Savior whose image they bare a likeness to? Could that question have any bearing on why that anonymous image was created? Who was the model for this image when the bible describes someone totally different? I wonder how many Black people have questioned this same issue in their own minds. There is even the infamous shroud of Turin that is said to be the death shroud of Jesus Christ and bares the imprint of his face and wounds upon its fabric. Over the years, millions have traveled to witness this artifact. But again, the image on the shroud is of the same likeness that covers our fans and crucifixes and is in conflict with the description in the bible. Recently, on morning news program, 'The Today's Show', a brief news report regarding the 'Shroud of Turin' was profiled. One of the historians interviewed regarding the shroud stated, in justifying this image, "Many of the people of this time wore their hair long and adorned beards." I have a question; does lamb's wool hang straight down on the shoulders? Does that not contradict the description in the bible? Does it make any difference to anyone that carbon tests have shown the shroud to only be about 600 years old? If you would stop a moment and look around the world, most other cultures worship Saviors, Messengers or even Gods that reflect their own image. We, as Black Americans, as well as Catholics, Protestants and Methodists all over the world, have been force-fed and have digested this incorrect image and

If Not Now, When?

simply accepted it as so despite the description in the very book that tells HIS story. Why is there no major mention of Black people in the bible? Could it have been that almost everyone involved in the "Greatest Story Ever Told" were people of color? Let's take a look at the region and time frame where much of the bible took place. Let us study the Hamitic Scriptures. Weren't Moses, Solomon, John, Peter, Mary Magdalen, the Pharaohs, and Noah, to name a few, all people of color? The legendary beauty of Cleopatra was not the same as the beauty of Elizabeth Taylor, even though some historians have cited her as being of Greek descent despite the trail of African blood that ran through her veins.

If you want your preaching to be effective in the Revolution for the Evolution of Black People in America, then preach the truth! Yes, we hear you preach of the violence that flourishes in our inner cities and the sinful ways of the growing homosexual community. But, what and where is the origin of that violence and what has spurred the increasing outbreak of homosexuality amongst our youth?

You should preach about the wonders of our people. You should preach about the things that should make us proud to be black. You should create a nationwide campaign to teach and preach the truth and promote black independence within our communities. Can you truthfully teach and preach about the evolution of religion in the world without teaching and preaching about the Black man. Why is it a secret that three of the first Popes were men of color. Forget being politically correct. Or maybe the benefits of your position restrict you from going against the grain of mainstream society? Is it easier to preach the same sermons that we have been fed for over four hundred years and get rich individually, or is it too dangerous to break the mold and change in mid-stream to the truth? After all, Malcolm and Martin were murdered for their convictions and the power in their revised messages.

Where is the conviction for the truth? It appears that there is more conviction to making money. It puzzles me, (again, this is my own opinion) why so many of my people flock to these huge mega-churches and tithe great amounts of their income to a man, not without sin, who virtually sets upon a throne and resides over them and then drives his expensive car home to his gated mansion. To me that is as close to idolatry as you can get. This problem became clear to me some years ago when I was invited to go to this particular church in Newark, N.J.. It was a small church in the middle of a ghetto residential block. The very first thing that I noticed about this church was the big, shiny brand new Cadillac parked on the sidewalk right outside the church door. The second thing that I noticed was the large amount of poor old Black women marching up the hill with their canes and having to maneuver around this big shiny Cadillac in order to get inside the church. Once I got inside the church I observed that there were only two types of people in the congregation of this church: they were poor old Black women and young children. You could count the amount of men on one hand and people between the ages of fifteen and forty were virtually non-existent.

The minister emerged from the back room, approached the pulpit in his glorious robe and led the church in song. Now, I hadn't been to church in many, many years, so I didn't know the words to these hymns. But I stood along with everyone else and rocked back and forth with the beat. This same act I repeated every time he requested a hymn. Once he began his sermon, he stopped mid-sentence and stated that he had been compelled to address another issue. Now this event happened in the late seventies to early eighties and it was during a phase in my life when hustling and being a player was what I was about. So here I am sitting in this poor church with a silk-sharkskin suit and some eel-skin shoes trying to figure out where this minister was going. He suddenly bellowed out, "Don't think that you are too cool to sing the praises of the Lord! Don't think that you are dressed too fine to celebrate in His Glory!"

I looked around the church to see to whom he was directing his message. It did not take too long for me to realize that most of these women were so poor that they had only house dresses or shift dresses on and the few old men that were present had on suits that they probably owned since 1946. That left me. Silk sharkskin, eel skin, dangling gold earring and all. I began to feel self conscious because he was really beginning to carry on in his impromptu sermon. He got louder and louder and started to dance about. It was getting hot and heavy and he began to come out of his robe. At that exact point I saw it. I was taken totally aback. He had on a suit that put mine to shame and a pair of Maury Gators! Those are twelve hundred dollar shoes! Now I am starting to really notice all of the diamonds on his fingers and wrist and the huge gold medallion around his neck. The gall! The hypocrisy! The out and out balls! Here he is ordering the passing of the plate every twenty minutes during this three hour service, taking money from these old poor people on fixed incomes and he's wearing twelve hundred dollar shoes! I also deducted that it was his big, shiny, brand new Cadillac blocking the front door up on the sidewalk.

That self-conscious feeling that I had before left my body and anger replaced it. The emotional anger I felt was so intense tears welled in my eyes. Without further hesitation, I rose and walked out.

> *"You cannot serve people by giving them orders as to what to do. The real servant of the people must live among them, think with them, feel for them and die for them."*
>
> *The servant of the people, unlike the leader, is not on a high horse elevated above the people and trying to carry them to some designated point to which he would like to go for his advantage. The servant of the people is down among them, living as they live, doing what they do and enjoying what they enjoy. He may be a little better informed than some other members of the group; it may be that he has had some experience that they have not had, but in spite of this advantage he should have more humility than those whom he serves, for we are told that "Whosoever is greatest among you, let him be your servant."*
>
> *Carter G. Woodson, 1933*

Here it is almost thirty years later and I am witnessing the same thing. Only now it is on a much larger scale. The big, shiny Cadillacs have been replaced by Bentleys and Rolls Royces. The nice suits have been replaced by custom tailored outfits, and the gold has turned to platinum. Let's not even mention the shoes. People flock to these men, (I repeat) who are not free of sin, and virtually worship their every word. The key term here is 'men'. They are no different than you or I; they have just been given the gift of gab. What they preach is the same as what any other man or woman who read the bible would teach, his interpretation of the word. Plus there is the fact that his interpretation is based on what he learned from the establishment founded by those who oppressed us. Throw in their little individual twists and you have a solid 'money-maker'.

They can not walk on water, part the water or turn the water to wine, so why do we bestow so much praise on them.

I am sure that many people will come to their defense and tell of all the good things that they do in their communities. I wouldn't dispute that they do accomplish some good things. However, imagine how much more they could do if they weren't living in such excess. What more could they do if they simply lived in a modest five hundred thousand dollar home instead of a five million dollar home. That's 4.5 million dollars that could go back into the community! Maybe if they drove a brand new Ford or Chevy, even a Lincoln, instead of a Bentley they could live and commune amongst their congregation. They live like rock stars instead of men of GOD. Is that GOD's message to the masses? Are we to accumulate as much material 'stuff' as humanly possible? Can we actually buy salvation? Let's take a moment to consider some of the damage these mega-churches are doing. First, let's examine the lost of true fellowship among members of these communities. People come from miles away and many different communities in search of a man to help them pray for riches. With 20,000 members, you never even get to meet or fellowship with the majority of them. Many members of these churches have attended for years and have never shook the hand of the man they so avidly support. So these mega-church preachers delegate ministries to handle the issues, sicknesses, blessings, marriages and funerals of their congregations. Maybe the head of some of these ministries should have their own church since they do so much ministering. Next, let's examine the capitalistic individualism that is being promoted. These churches cater only to those people who can afford to attend and tithe ten percent of their income. Do the poor people surviving from paycheck to paycheck or from government check to government check not need salvation. Along with the lost of fellowship, we are also loosing our sense of community. The village mentality, which brought us through slavery, 'Jim Crow' and the racism and discrimination of the 50s and 60s is being pushed further and further out of our existence. Consequently, black people in America are steadily becoming a fractured race striving for individual riches instead of real wealth as a people. Mega-churches are not new, white people started this phenomenon many years ago. When I was a child there was Billy Graham and Jimmy Swaggart, to name a couple, and let's not forget the Granddaddy of them all, the Catholic Church. Black folks have now caught on and are beginning to come into their own. Again, the assimilation into this white/European capitalistic way of life is stripping us of our naturalness and tearing us farther apart as a race. A race that, no matter what amount of individual riches we accrue, still holds second-class citizenship in this country.

Someone please explain to me why a minister needs bodyguards? Even better, why does the Pope ride in a bulletproof bubble. What does that tell us about his faith? If they are preaching and living the truth and the word of GOD, what is it they fear. Will GOD not protect them? Do they not believe that when GOD calls them that there is not a bodyguard or a vehicle that can protect them? I thought that to sit at the foot of the throne in righteousness was the ultimate reward. Tell me, what are they afraid of? The only things that they have to lose are their earthly possessions. Their righteous soul will live on in the eternal, won't it? Isn't that what they always taught in Sunday school and church?

The number of black religious leaders who supported President Bush's re-election campaign also confused me. He based his political forum on morality and ethics at the same time he was waging war on a people that were innocent of the crime that was committed that gave us grounds for war in the first place. He openly and blatantly deceived the American public and committed thousands upon thousands of our young men and women to be murdered and maimed in a war that even hindsight tells us cannot be won. Instead of relentlessly pursuing the real known culprits of the heinous crime of September 11, 2001, he simply diverted to pursue an old foe that presented no immediate danger to us. Now, five years later, the American people are at bay of a constant threat that is running free to threaten or attack us at any given moment.

So engulfed in this political ploy of distractions, a Georgia religious leader marched his congregation to the MLK memorial center against homosexual unions (a major campaign issue) at the same time a law was being passed to block and arrest homeless people from begging in downtown Atlanta. Now, I could be wrong, but I don't ever recall hearing of a gay terrorist group threatening the American people or a homeless terrorist group for that matter. Also, there is not one single homosexual couple, group or individual who can come between, or affect, in any way, the relationship between my wife and I. The reason that our religious leaders fell so gullibly for this ploy befuddled me until I read several articles in some popular magazines. The Bush administration had held conference with many Black religious leaders and offered them conditional considerations, in return for the support of their congregations. And we, despite what is plainly in our faces, followed our religious leaders in support of these deceptions.

Despite the economic state and failing school systems of our communities, despite the swiftly increasing unemployment rates amongst our people and the critical state of the killer AIDS virus in our communities, we blindly followed our leaders like a flock of lost sheep for causes that do not affect our people. The President made no promises of addressing our immediate or future problems.

One of his major platforms was the war on homosexuality. Homosexuality is not a disease that we can cure. It is not a problem that we can fix. We could outlaw it and it will simply go back underground and behind close doors like it was in the forties and fifties. We could arrest every gay man and woman we see and we would simply have prisons and jails overcrowded and overrun with homosexual activity, as if it is not bad enough. Homosexuality is not tearing at the fiber of the institution of marriage. This nihilistic patriarchal society is. The well established double-standard between men and women in regards to infidelity and the capitalistic standard of what makes a man in this country is what threatens the institution of marriage. It is almost laughable to me that our religious leaders so ardently condemn homosexuals, yet they accept their tithes and allow them to lead and participate in their choirs. How many really fantastic choirs have you heard where some openly gay participants are not some of the loudest, liveliest and most talented voices to be heard. Some of the most creative professions in the world are dominated by gay individuals. Is there something to be said about a person who is not struggling to establish his manhood that leaves them free to express their creativity? Please don't get me wrong. I am in no way defending or promoting homosexuality. However, the simple truth is that it has been here for as long as man has recorded his history and it will be here long after you or I have gone. So why does it take precedent over homelessness, unemployment, home security, hunger and ill-fated war. All Americans have been bamboozled and some of our most powerful religious leaders have helped to lead us there. I agree that there should be a campaign to address homosexuality, but it should not take precedent over the things that affect us all everyday. A war against homosexuality can be compared to the war in Iraq; both are ill fated and cannot be won. If indeed homosexuality is a sin, then GOD Himself will stand in judgment.

What we need from our religious leaders are combined efforts in major campaigns against the state of the educational systems in our communities and major pushes for the empowerment and independence of our neighborhoods. We need campaigns for the empowerment of minority business owners and since so many of our religious leaders have proven to be such astute and successful businessmen, maybe they should teach some of our people how to be successful in their respective businesses in return for a commitment to their respective communities. What we need from our religious leaders is the truth and how spirituality and religion relates to us as a people. To those who are brave enough to tell the truth, I tip my hat and applaud your courage.

To my people who so diligently support these men of material excess, I have a question. Do you consider your tithes as a mandatory sacrifice of your earnings to be stored in some temple to appease a god that needs money? Or is it the same as supporting your local grocer or pharmacist? Is it like simply trading currency for the service of supplying you with bread, milk and medicine? I understand the concept of paying the salary of your local minister for his services and I understand the more the merrier. But are his services rendered to make a buck or to support and help the community and lead souls to salvation? It seems to me that you are paying a mere mortal (again, not without sin) an excessive amount of money to deliver the message of a carpenter who delivered HIS message in tattered clothe and worn sandals. With a congregation of sometimes upwards of 20,000 footing his bills, when you are alone in meditation and your heart is troubled in the night, can you call on him for some guidance and foresight? Does he even know you name?

There is so much wrong with the world today and it seems that everyone has their own separate agenda. The sad truth is that very, very few of those separate agenda involve delivering our world to salvation. Most are really thinking of themselves. Many of them are not really concerned with salvation, they are just trying to get as much material 'stuff' as they can while they are here. I just recently read an article in the Atlanta Journal Constitution on Sunday, January 29, 2006 that another Mega-Church minister has been charged with scandal. He has been charged with coercing some of his female followers to commit sexual favors and has been doing this for decades. Corruption is rampant in all aspects of American life. Far too many priest and ministers are found to be guilty of fornication, infidelity, homosexuality and pedophilia. Far too many have also amassed great fortunes only to be revealed as con men and grifters. The 'Call' to spread the word of GOD is suppose to be a 'high calling' to those whose hearts are worthy and true. How do we know the difference between the 'gifted' and the 'grifters'? How do we know who is pure and true at heart? Maybe if the material reward were not so great, we might not have as many imposters and con men trying their luck at the craft.

> *"In the Black World, the Preacher and Teacher embodied once the ideals of this people, -the strife for another and a juster world, the vague dream of righteousness, the mystery of knowing; but today the danger is that these ideals, with their simple beauty and weird inspiration, will suddenly sink to a question of cash and a lust for gold. "*
>
> *W.E.B. Dubois, The Souls of Black Folk, 1893*

To those who are true at heart, I challenge you to call out all who bear false witness. I challenge you all to banish all false images from your churches, temples, homes and hearts. I challenge you to call for a ban of all displays of that false image from every fan, bookmark, Sunday school book and all other depictions that misrepresent the image described in the Bible. Shout out the truth from the hilltops! Redirect your mission from the amassing of riches to the saving of souls. Inspire young future ministers and preachers not with the material gains that the position of leadership offers, but with the integrity, trustworthiness and humility of a man who is slave to nothing and no one and who serves only GOD.

Throughout history each society or civilization has had its own agenda and that is one of the reasons that we have so many 'truths'. The real truth has been spread so thin it has become easier and easier to variate and customize. Each society has created a religion that supported their particular agenda. These religions have been passed down through generations and generations, over centuries and have evolved into the many religions that we see throughout the world today. Many societies have used religion to justify religious wars, ethnic cleansing, slavery, condemnation and genocide all in the name of God.

Religion is a man-made process and it serves a particular purpose. One of the main purposes of religion is mass control. It was imperative for the founders and rulers of these societies to establish a right way, and a wrong way of thinking. It was imperative to create a format that was stronger than man-made laws. Appealing to the spirit, moral instincts and the soul of the citizenry of those particular societies proved most effective; even the political strategist of President George W. Bush knew that.

In simpler words, you can justify just about anything when you claim that God is on your side.

Spirituality, on the other hand, is an individual experience. I personally, don't believe that spirituality can be taught or given to someone. I believe everyone is born with the spirit. At some point, (a point that is different for every individual) an individual's life will be ready to acknowledge and claim that spirit and at that time he or she will search out methods and means to release the power of that spirit. This release may come through the church, fellowshipping, or spreading the Gospel. It might come through volunteer work or missionary work; it might even just simply change an individual's life from a life of sin and strife, to a life of peace and tranquility. No matter what the outcome or effect, it is all based on that person's individual relationship with God.

As stated earlier in this book, the mind is a very complicated tool as well as a weapon. Once the mind has decided to open up and receive a leader or Shepard, it is prone to accept and justify just about anything that leader says. This occurs even when there are obvious warning signs of unworthiness. This is not a new revelation; this is human nature. How did Jim Jones convince all those people to drink poison kool-aid or David Carress convince those men, women and children to take up arms at Waco, Texas?

We are all 'suckers' for a good line. But, I believe that our inner spirit is smarter than we are. If we could just tap into it, release it, follow it and let the spirit lead us we would find a better way.

VII.
A message to all entertainers and athletes:

Whether you are willing to accept, acknowledge or receive it or not, you are all role models. You have excelled with excellence to the top of your individual crafts. You have conquered all of the obstacles that confront our people and risen to a level that we all aspire to. Your accomplishments establish a standard that inspires every one of your fans. Your lives and actions have been placed in an open book for all to see. We, your fans, sit back and watch you grow. You are the example that proves to us all that we can make it no matter what the odds. Our children emulate your every action. They want to run like you, shoot like you, throw like you, sing and dance like you. 'They want to be like Mike'. They emulate you even down to your mistakes and misgivings.

I stated earlier in this book that every Black man and woman is a role model and an icon to their people. But, professional athletes and entertainers are at the fore-front because of your visibility. Everyone wants praise and respect for what they accomplish, whether it be on the field, on the court, on the stage or in the office or at home. The praise and respect you get pays your salary. It is your responsibility as a member of a race of people that has been down trodden and is struggling to gain ground, to inspire and nurture our children and to spur them on to greater aspirations than even you have achieved. Our children, as well as the adults, who pay to see you need to see and hear your story from your mouths. We need to know your struggles, your failures and your triumphs. Our children need to know what kind of dedication, sacrifice and discipline it takes to achieve your level of success. They need to know what you do during the off-season to prepare yourself for the future. They need to know how you prepare yourself for the future when your body will no longer allow you to compete with the younger, stronger and faster incoming superstars. The children need to know what part did your education play in your professional and private life. They need to know where you came from and the origin of your inspiration.

We as a people need all of the help and inspiration that we can get and we need it most from those of us who have achieved the things that we dream about. We need to learn to respect the sacrifices of those before us who paved the way and set the standards for us to surpass. Today, unlike the 50s and 60s, we as a people lack the premiere leadership of a Martin Luther King or Malcolm X. Therefore, those of us who are conscious and aware with a leg up must grab the reins and pull the wagon along until a courageous and inspired leader emerges to lead us further down the path. Even then we cannot stop because he or she will have a tough time motivating a people that has been virtually leaderless for nearly half a century.

Athletes and entertainers who fall to the wayside, just as we need the successful superstars to come and talk to the children, we need you also. The children need to hear about where you went wrong and how to get back up from a major let down. If drugs were your downfall, they need to hear just how you became enticed and how did it affect your performance, your thinking and your future. They need to know what they can do to avoid such pitfalls. What I am trying to say is that we need everybody to participate in this revolution. Hopefully, we can avoid a revolution with guns and violence. This is not a revolution against anyone else, it is a revolution against our invisible enemy. This is a revolution designed to destroy the failing side of ourselves and take our people to the next level. Hopefully it

If Not Now, When?

will evolve into a momentum that will carry on for generations to come.

Hip-Hop and R&B artists;

Your influence has the greatest power and range of all amongst the young people of the world. Your message reaches corners that we cannot even see. It reaches across borders, across the seas, across all barriers and color lines. It is omnipresent all over the globe. Your message is most important because of your target audience; the young people. The future diplomats and lawmakers, doctors and teachers, governors and presidents listen to your lyrics and beats everyday, all day long. You, whether you want to be or not, are an integral part of the success of this revolution. Your lyrics and music incite, inspire and enthrall your audience with a power that is uncanny. It is unlike any music genre ever. In my generation we were amazed at the effect the Beatles had on the world; your music blanks that occurrence totally out. To put it in a visual, witnessing the effect of your music is like watching the whole world do the 'Electric Slide' to one beat.

There are some Hip Hop artist that I feel have a grasp of the power that they hold, like Common, KRS-One and Floetry. I don't think that most do. I get the feeling that for many of them, it is just entertainment that they get paid for. For some it is just a fantasy. They rap about a life they've only heard about. I have to wonder if they really, really realize how much they sway the minds and actions of the young people all over the world. The effects of the Hip Hop persuasion are evident everywhere. From the Americas to China, from Africa to Russia, the phenomenon has children and young adults wearing sagging pants, oversized T-shirts and twisted ball caps. The Hip Hop language has ascended all barriers. The overall influence is unprecedented.

Today, for the first time in African American history, we have the ear of the world. Not because of some special event. Not because one or two men have risen above normal consciousness or there's been a major riot, instead it is because our people have ushered in a new genre of communication that has taken the world by storm. But now that we have the world by the ear, what are we telling them? Well, we are telling them that some of our brightest stars are going to prison in droves. We are telling the world that some of our most talented prospects are thugs, gangsters and sex addicts. We are telling them that although we may not be able to capitalize on industrialization, we surely can cap our teeth with gold and platinum and we may not be buying land for investment, but we are buying spinners for our Land Rovers, Hummers, BMWs and Mercedes. Again, I say that there is nothing wrong with pursuing and obtaining the finer things in life, it just should not be our highest priority; Black Power should.

There is a distinct difference between a young Caucasian kid from a well-to-do community buying a eighty thousand dollar car and a young black kid, straight out of the projects, who has come into some money and that's the first thing that he wants to buy. That white kid doesn't have to worry about his community or the people trapped there, his people, as a whole, and his community is thriving and prospering. On the other hand, the kid from the project or ghetto hails from a community full of despair, desperation and are in dire need of salvation. It must be his responsibility, as well as everyone else's, to help save his community and his people. I personally know that it is hard for the average Joe when he is simply working hard to make a better way of life for his family, but there are a few of us who are gifted with blessings and run straight for the hills. When we receive those blessings, we should share those blessings with our communities by purchasing property, businesses and creating jobs opportunities for ourselves. It is not impossible, people from outside our communities come into our communities and do it all the time, and very successfully, I might add.

We, as a people, have indeed made many gains in this society and we have opened many doors that, in the past, have been closed to us. That is a very good thing. The problem lies in the fact that many of us don't consider those gains the gains of a people. Unfortunately, some of those non-believers are the very people making some of those gains. They think in terms of "I got mines, now you get yours". That is the Lynch Letter effect hard at work still. As a subjugated people, every inch gained should be celebrated and nailed into place as if it is a rung in the ladder to the next level. We should not forget those who created those gains and they should not forget us.

While we have the ears of the world, we should alert them that we are on the way. They should not fear that we might 'jack' them, rather, they should fear the power in our resolve, the power in our knowledge and abilities and the power in our civility. After all, we are the

If Not Now, When?

descendants of the original people who created the first civilization. So, my young Hip Hop impresarios, I know and understand your message of anger and despair. I am a survivor of 'The Life'. I hail from the same depths that you rap about. But rapping about what we see and do everyday means nothing. The time for talking, singing, praying, meetings and marches are over. We have come a long way, but we still have a longer way to go. It is time for action. It is time for revolution.

I participated in my own way with the million-man march. I watched as a million or so men and boys gathered together to announce a stand. The message was clear and strong. But, when the gathering was over, so was the stand. We all went right back to what we were doing before the march. I saw a million or so hands raised high in the air with dollars clinched in their fists. Some had one-dollar bills, others held up fives and tens and some with twenties and fifties. I personally, have no idea where that money went. I am not saying that it wasn't used for good causes, I am simply saying that myself, as well as many others with whom I have spoken, have not seen the evidence of that powerful display of rare unity.

Just as there are press conferences when a Black man commits a heinous crime, there should be a press conference when Black people have crossed another divide or achieved another potent gain. The aftermath of the Million-Man March should have been publicized or broadcasted for all to see and hear. The results from the contributions given should have been announced. Maybe if some major good were done with those contributions it would inspire us all to do more, more often. We must become more accountable for our actions and we must also account for the efforts of those who sacrifice for change.

I would love to hear about the Black owned private schools that are so desperately needed in our communities, that is offering scholarships to those who can't afford to attend but qualify academically and curriculums that involve topics that we as a people sorely need to survive, compete and excel. We need curriculums that concentrate on black achievement throughout world history for inspiration and affirmation of our place in this universe. We need to prop up our young people and show them the importance of their part in this revolution.

We, as a people, are not capitalizing on obvious opportunities to act on issues that affect us daily. We are not proactive against the occurrences that will inevitably dictate our near or distant futures. Our people are on a steady downward spiral. There are some who would argue that we are making progress every day. The truth is that there are individuals who are making significant individual gains, but, as a people, we are constantly losing the respect of the world. Truth in point, the President of Mexico stated clearly that the successful onslaught of Mexican immigration into the United States is supported by the fact that the immigrants are willing to do the jobs that American Blacks refuse to do. If we are suffering from poverty and homelessness, unemployment and despair, how could there possibly be a job that we won't do? Although the vast majority of Black Americans are hard working, GOD-fearing and law abiding citizens, the truth of the matter is that there are indeed many, many young people who refuse to do the menial, low paying jobs that do exist in abundance.

My parents instilled a solid work ethic in me at a very young age. We were, beyond a doubt, a poor family, but we learned that there were rewards for a job well done, no matter how small they may be, rewards all the same. Many of us are spoiling our kids by providing them with every possible luxury from one hundred dollar sneakers to expensive electronic equipment. All the while our children are performing at inadequate or sub-par levels. I remember many years ago, asking my mother for a pair of Chuck Taylor Converse All Star sneakers at the lofty price of $6.99. She looked at me like I was crazy, then she took me to the local supermarket and bought me a pair of those sneakers with the tough string that held the pair together and hung on a rack next to the bread. Needless to say, I felt the need to work at a very young age. My very first official job was sweeping up hair at the corner barbershop on Ridgewood and Madison Avenues at the tender age of ten. I was extremely proud then and I am still proud of that to this day. I eventually saved up enough money to buy my own first pair of Chuck Taylor All Stars. Even as an adult I find that there is a personal gratification to collecting a check for a hard days work and paying your own way.

VIII
Young Black People

I know that the generation before has failed you in many ways. I do not, and cannot consciously blame you for the state of our people or our world. You have inherited a world full of problems and we have not given you the tools, knowledge or wisdom to deal with the many issues that have befallen you. We have not even equipped you with a base in which to start. Yes, we have failed you indeed. We have forgotten what the leaders of our generation had taught us and neglected to pass on to you the methods and convictions of all our leaders from the past. I am here to take the blame for my generation and our failures. Now, what's next?

I have hereby resolved the 'blame-game'. Now we must move toward resolution. We must come together, young and old, lower class, middle class and upper class, to create and commit to this revolution together. We must commit to accomplishing this task with as little or as many casualties as it will take.

Throughout this book I have used the words we, our, I and my. I cannot possibly separate myself as if I have no guilt in this matter. I am you and that is why I am so passionate about this subject. We are letting ourselves down. Mr. Cosby puts the blame on the people of the lower classes as if we are purposely self destructing ourselves. We did have help getting to the point that we are. The problem also weighs on the upper classes. I am talking about the people who have become successes, but have not reached back down to pull the masses up from the depths of desperation.

> "I shall never stop practicing philosophy and exhorting you and elucidating the truth for everyone that I meet. I shall go on saying...Are you not ashamed that you give your attention to acquiring as much money as possible, and similarly with reputation and honor and give no attention to truth and understanding and the perfection of your soul?...I shall do this to everyone I meet, young or old, foreigner or fellow citizen, but especially to you, my fellow citizens.
>
> -Socrates, from Plato's Apology 29d-30a

I agree that there are too few of us that are using our torrid past as a propellant to jettison ourselves forward. Many of us use it as a crutch and a reason to lay back and sulk. Anger is a useless emotion that should be addressed and converted into positive energy. An individual who holds onto anger in its original state will eventually lash out in emotional chaos or wallow in the depressive darkness of negativity. If you look at our history here in the United States, you will see our people holding onto that anger and either lashing out at ourselves or wallowing in negativity or both. As individuals we are amassing great fortunes and great amounts of 'stuff'. As a people, we are losing ground. We are losing the respect of the world. Other minority groups are growing in leaps and bounds. Between abortions, rising infant mortality rates, AIDS, incarceration, homosexuality and genocide, the writing is on the wall. Black America, as we know it is headed for extinction. Within our lifetime the Latin and Hispanic community will overtake us as the majority minority. As fast as we are dying they are multiplying, working hard and building vast communities all over the country.

One of the most obvious things that hold us back is our inability to work together. Again, whether we recognize it or not, the Lynch Letter is hard at work, even in the new millennium. There was a distinct plan to train us away from one another by discouraging us

If Not Now, When?

from doing anything other than working in the fields and practicing the religion the way they taught it to us. This was accomplished by beating, torturing and/or hanging anyone who conspired to help another slave outside of those boundaries. These beatings and hangings were done in front of all of the slaves in effort to teach a mass lesson of discouragement against standing up as a people. It worked then and it is still working today.

When I was a young boy I had a friend. He was Haitian. He had been to my home many times, but he never, ever invited me to his home. I thought that maybe it was because his family was so poor and he was embarrassed. Well, I was half right. As we grew up and went our separate ways, I ran into him and he revealed that indeed he was embarrassed. But, the reason was because he had almost twenty-five adult relatives all living in a two-bedroom apartment. This was back in the mid sixties and each one of those relatives in that apartment had at least two jobs. They all pooled their incomes together and soon they bought an entire apartment building. They then proceeded to fill the new apartment building with friends and relatives from back home in Haiti. They all went out and found jobs, pooled their incomes together and bought a cabstand. Then they bought a candy store, then a drug store and then some more apartment buildings. Within ten years they practically owned an entire city block and are putting their children through medical and engineering schools.

Those people have come here to this country from very poor countries, worked very hard and amassed a commendable amount of wealth and created their own communities. I applaud their accomplishments. I have witnessed very similar strategies among the Hispanic communities. During the 1980s, I worked with some Hispanic men and women in a chemical plant in the Ironbound section of East Newark, New Jersey. I befriended one particular gentleman who invited me to his home for lunch. In his home I found so very many things that represented his culture and traditions. But the main thing that I noticed was how uniquely designed and beautiful his home was structured. I was curious and I asked, "you make the same money as I do, so how can you afford to have all this work done on your home?" He replied in his Hispanic accent, "Ezz very simple. My neighbor next door does masonry work and the guy across the street does carpentry and I do electrician work. I re-wire his home and in-turn, he built a new deck for me. We then got together and completely finished my other neighbors basement and in return, he built us both beautiful brick and cement porches. So for very little money and a little hard work, all three of our families have beautiful homes to live in."

It almost amazes me, (note I said 'almost') that people can come from such poor countries and create such decent lives here when it seems that American Blacks can't seem to get pass 'boys in the hood'. The reason why it does not fully amaze me is because I know a major part of the reason why. We are still victim of the mis-treatment and the mis-education of the American Black man. Although many other people have been enslaved and even persecuted throughout world history, no other people were totally stripped of their culture, language, land, religion and traditions, then taken to a foreign place and subjected to the horrors that the American Black man has. It was as if an entire race of people had been kidnapped and brainwashed. In the book, "The Debt", by activist Randall Robinson, he captures a quote by Edward Blyden in 1903;

> *Every race has a soul, and the soul of that race finds expression in its institutions, and to kill those institutions is to kill the soul...No people can profit or be helped under institutions, which are not the outcome of their own character.*
>
> *(Robinson, 2000)*

The de-brainwashing of an entire race of people has proven to be a virtually impossible undertaking especially when the powers that control the resources can find no benefit in doing so. This leaves the de-brainwashing to the few people who were strong enough to free themselves of their mental prison. So many of the masses cannot be reached and so many others have been blinded and pacified with material 'stuff' and see nothing wrong. I have spoken with many people from foreign countries that are much more poorer than ours and they cannot understand why the American Black man lives and acts the way he does in such a 'so-called' great country.

What fully amazes me is why this country does not realize that if it embraces and tends to all of its citizens, how much more powerful it would be. Why does this country not realize that the race to be the undisputedly greatest country in the world is to be won through the strength and efficiency of the education of its young people. Other countries like Japan, China and India realize this and they concentrate and invest in the strict education of their young people. This is evident in their meteoric rise in science, technology and medicine.

The quality of life is disintegrating for the middle and lower class Americans. Crime corruption and depravity are raging in this country and not just among those who live below the poverty level. Although homosexuality is growing at an alarming rate all over the world and especially here in this country, it is only a part of the deterioration of the morality. What is worse is the constant and growing victimization of defenseless children by pedophiles who are protected or cloaked by some powerful religious Reich or belong to some wealthy social club or organization like the 'Man-Boy' club. It is also the fact that no one notices the many tons of cocaine, heroin and marijuana that fly into this country everyday until it reaches some young black boys pocket. It is the fact that the penalty for possessing a gram of crack cocaine is more severe than for possessing an ounce of powder cocaine. When you consider the demographics of that scenario, then you will understand the ridiculousness of it. Who is most likely to possess an ounce of powder cocaine versus who is most likely to possess a gram of crack? There are literally thousands of these small inequalities that tear at the fiber of this country.

I understand the concept behind a 'civilized society'. I also understand that in order to maintain a civilized society there must be law and order. In keeping order, there must law enforcement and a penalty system that punishes those who violate the laws of that particular society. Without those things a civilized society would devolve into uncivilized chaos.

I am a believer in, but not a supporter of, capital punishment. Let me explain that conundrum. I believe in an "eye for a eye". There are criminals who actually commit crimes with such depraved indifference that they pose an immediate danger to virtually everyone they come in contact with from civilians, to law enforcement, to prison guards and even to fellow inmates. Although a person like this may receive a life sentence or even consecutive life sentences he or she may still present a danger to all that have contact with him or her.

It is the leader of a civilized society who bears the responsibility of protecting the citizens of that community. Sometimes the protection of a community as a whole supersedes the preservation of a single life that threatens the quality of life in that community. I personally favor the old 'Baghdad Rule': "If you get caught stealing, we cannot guarantee that you won't steal again, however, we can guarantee that you won't steal with that hand again." As you might guess, the crime rate is much lower over there. I don't believe that our method of capital punishment is a deterrent. One reason is that the criminals in our society are far removed from the actual event of execution. None of them have actually seen an execution except on television. Many other countries still perform their executions in a public forum for all to see. In my opinion that would be more effective.

The second reason is that the one part of the death sentence that our resident criminals do see is the constant 'stays of execution' and the incredible length of time that an inmate can end up staying on death row, sometimes in excess of twenty years!

I truly believe that some crimes are so heinous and depraved that the offender deserves immediate and complete extermination so as to ensure that the community is safe from him or her. People are getting crazier by the minute and so should the punishment. Why should we be concerned with the humanity of the extermination of a person who murders an expectant mother and then viciously cuts the baby from her womb? This person is seriously warped and you think someone can cure him or her?

That is how I feel emotionally. However, in a civilized society we cannot allow our emotions to dictate the rules and law. In this society in particular, we must concern ourselves with the facts and think critically. Because of the facts I could not possibly support or condone capital punishment in this country. This country has grown up with racist discrimination and inequalities running all through its bloodstream. The statistics on the percentage of people of color who have been executed, whether by electric chair, lethal injection or lynching, throughout the history of America, screams out for attention. From day one our people have been persecuted unfairly. For whistling at a white woman, young Emmett Till was beaten and shot, at a time when white men whistled at, lusted for, and raped our women without retribution. In Texas Mr. James Byrd was tied to the back of a pickup truck and dragged down the street until he was decapitated simply for the crime of being black. Mumia Abu-Jamal was jailed and sentence to death for a crime that could not possibly be proven without reasonable doubt. Reuben Hurricane Carter spent a relative lifetime in prison for a crime that he was obviously framed for.

In Georgia alone, in less than six years, no less than six black men were freed from prison after spending combined sentences of more than 100 years behind bars for crimes of rape that they have been exonerated from. Robert Clark Jr. served twenty-five years for raping a white woman who picked him out of a line up and never wavered in her identification. While imprisoned he campaigned for his innocence and even told the authorities who the real culprit was. They ignored his pleas, kept him in prison and allowed the real rapist to run free to rape again. Twenty-five years later, DNA proved his innocence and he was freed in December 2005. His accuser later apologized for her mistake. Mr. Calvin Johnson, under similar circumstances, was sentenced to life for the same type of crime. Sixteen years later, thanks to DNA, he was also freed. It took seventeen years for Mr. Clarence Harrison to be freed of a crime he did not commit. Samuel Scott and Douglas Echols were both charged with kidnapping, rape and robbery in 1986. Mr. Scott received life plus twenty years and Mr. Echols served time and was given ten years probation and labeled as a sex offender. In 2001 DNA excluded both men in the rape. Also note that in 2001 Mr. Scott was released on parole, arrested two days later for failing to register as a sex offender, released again on the electronic monitoring system, only to be jailed in 2002 for not being able to afford to pay the monthly electronic monitoring fee. In Virginia three more black men were recently exonerated of the crimes for which they were convicted: Marvin Anderson, Arthur Lee Whitfield and Julius Ruffin. If not for the foresight of a lab technician, Ms. Mary Jane Burton, (a white woman) and her hopes for a breakthrough in testing which compelled her to store and preserve some evidence which was later discovered, after her death, and submitted to DNA testing, these men would surely still be in prison. The list can go on and on.

The double standard between what has been labeled a 'white collar' crime vs. the common 'blue collar' crime speaks for itself. The 'powers that be' have created a separate category for the crimes that they are most guilty of, affording them a softer prison environment. The difference between a federal prison and a state prison equals the difference between the suburbs and the ghetto. A crime against this society is a crime against this society. If you don't want to be placed in a confined space with 'low-life' common criminals to be beaten up, raped and/or even murdered, then don't commit a crime. Yes, I do agree that the length of the sentence should match the severity of the crime, but a crime is still a crime. Should the capitalistic crime of embezzling millions of dollars from unsuspecting citizens of this society, possibly casting some into poverty, be met with a softer sentence than the young black boy capitalizing on the financial opportunity found in selling drugs? Should the construction engineer who goes into the homes of unsuspecting senior citizens and swindles them out of their entire life savings be treated differently than the young Hispanic man found guilty in a home invasion?

Should the devastation of a citizen who has contributed to the welfare of this country for an entire lifetime not be tantamount in the sentencing of this 'white collar' criminal? Should he not serve the same 'three hots and a cot' as the young black boy who sold an ounce of pot to someone who wanted to buy it? Of course he should. Instead, he gets to serve federal time in a state-of-the-art facility with libraries, tennis courts, swimming pools and color, cable television in his dormitory (uh, I mean cell).

No, I cannot support capital punishment or the justice system in this country even though my emotions scream for retribution against those who murder, especially children.

The above mentioned are among the many, many injustices and inequalities that we suffer as a people here in America. All of these things affect our people disproportionately and all of our young people need think about these things when they think about their lives and their future. When will we stand up and begin to take responsibility for our own welfare in this country.

IX.
Black Business

Although I speak harshly about our failures, I try not to neglect our successes. I applaud and support any black person who endeavors into business ownership legitimately. As I have stated several times throughout this book, we have many individuals who have amassed great fortunes in business, athletics and entertainment. We have shown that despite discrimination and racism that we can excel in any medium. People like Robert Johnson who sold BET to Viacom for four billion dollars and is also the owner of the Charlotte Bobcats (a professional basketball team), has real estate and hotel ownership and a jazz label. Don H. Barden, CEO of Majestic Star Casinos recently bought Trump Indiana Casino and Hotel for an estimated $253 million. He also owns casinos in Mississippi, Colorado and Las Vegas. Then there is Oprah who is now listed among the richest and most powerful women in America. Those are just a few examples. Yes indeed, we have proven our capabilities over and over again. The problem is that with our status in this country, we are doing fantastic work at different tables. We need the ability to bring all of that talent to one table and create something global.

Despite those proven attributes, we as a people still suffer and lag behind. Again, the purpose of the 'Lynch Letter' (whether reality or hoax) and our orientation into American society, is still affecting our mentality. In fact, in this regard, we are regressing. We, as a people are moving farther and farther away from each other. After the abolishment of slavery, prior to 'JimCrow' and other means and methods of discrimination, black people surged forward and created flourishing communities like Rosewood and Ochee, Florida. We gained political seats and educational status. Prejudice, resentment and fear of our abilities forced the racist oppressors to take action and put concerted effort into beating our people back down.

Greenwood, Oklahoma was a strong black community in the early 1900s. It boasted a population of approximately ten thousand black residents. It was a community comprised of hard working church going, industrious people who owned drug stores, blacksmith shops, grocery or general stores and other small businesses. Greenwood also had a good number of big businessmen and women like doctors, lawyers and investors, railroad owners and other entrepreneurs. It was nicknamed 'Black Wall Street'. Many of these people migrated west during the 'big oil rush' and settled in Greenwood, Oklahoma. The citizenship of this community consisted of many different types of black Americans from ex-slaves, free black immigrants and blacks who migrated with the Indians. Together they built from scratch a thriving little metropolis and were willing to die to protect it. Some of the residents of this community amassed great wealth and it benefited the growth of their community. In their community they controlled their politics, their school system and their economy. Unfortunately, Greenwood, like Rosewood, Ochee and other black communities flourished during the time of much unrest in the American society. The era surrounding World War I was a devastating period for white America and an even worst time for thriving black citizens trying and succeeding in making the best of the lie of '40 acres and a mule'. In Greenwood, a young white woman's claim of sexual assault by a black man was all that was needed to catapult a historical riot that burned that community to the ground. In fact, during 1919 alone there were more than two-dozen different race riots recorded across the nation. Every one of them were instigated and executed by white mobs against black communities. These communities proved

If Not Now, When?

that despite racism and discrimination that we can successfully create and sustain communities. We can institute and successfully run businesses large and small and that we can work together with courage and conviction.

In the book, 'The Mis-Education of the Negro', the author, Carter G. Woodson, noted at a time,

> *"When the free Negroes were advised a hundred years ago to go to Africa they replied that they would never separate themselves from the slave population of this country as they were brethren by the 'ties of consanguinity, of suffering and of wrong'."*

> *"When, again in 1816, free Negroes like Richard Allen, James Forten and Robert Purvis, were referred to as a foreign element whose social status might not be secure in this country, instead of permitting the colonizationists to shove them aside as criminals to be deported to a distant shore, they replied in no uncertain terms that this soil in America which gave them birth is their only true home. "Here their fathers fought, bled, and died for this country and here they intended to stay."*

(Woodson, 1933)

One of the main problems with the black man in America today is that there is no longer such conviction. The allegiance between brotherhood and the perseverance of our people has dwindled and shrunken into an allegiance to individualism and singular gain. In another excerpt from his book, Mr. Woodson quotes another free Negro from the 1800s, a Baptist preacher from Albany;

> *Who informed the colonizationists that, "the free Negroes would not permit their traducers to formulate a program for the race. You may go ahead with your plan to deport this element in order to make slavery secure, he warned; but the free Negroes will never emigrate to Africa. "We shall stay here and fight until the foul monster is crushed. Slavery must go."*

"Did I believe it would always continue, and that man to the end of time would be permitted with impunity to usurp the same undue authority over his fellow, I would disavow any allegiance or obligation I was under to my fellow creatures, or any submission that I owed to the laws of my country! I would deny the superintending power of divine Providence in the affairs of this life; I would ridicule the religion of the Savior of the world, and treat as the worst of men the ministers of the everlasting gospel; I would consider my Bible as a book of false and delusive fables, and commit it to the flames; nay, I would still go farther; I would at once confess myself an atheist, and deny the existence of a holy God."

(Woodson, 1933)

"No matter how much respect, no matter how much recognition, whites show towards me, as far as I'm concerned, as long as it is not shown to every one of our people in this country, it doesn't exist for me."

Malcolm X (1964)

Such commitment and dedication is tantamount in the revolution for the evolution of the black man in America. It would seem that the blindness of many of our successful people to the effect that their singularisms have on us as a people proves to be in favor of the powers-that-be. Those powers realize that individual riches here and there can be no challenge to a power structure that has been in place for several centuries and controls the economy of this country.

Now, I may not know everything that goes on behind closed doors, but, I don't see my people thinking in terms of Wal-Mart, the 'box store' chain or General Mills or even Toyota. Those endeavors would take cooperation and cohesiveness. Those are two words that ring taboo amongst our people. We, as a people, cannot even agree on whom to vote for that would benefit us. Why should there even be a discrepancy when neither party truly does anything for us. They promise better school systems with "No Child Left Behind" and there are children left behind every day, especially our innocent poor black children. They promise to reduce unemployment and bring jobs to our communities and statistics still show that in some months as many as 100,000 jobs are lost. Black conservatives support capitalist ideas and bask in the individual gains that this American society affords them. But, if another depression or civil war should occur in this country, they would find themselves 'just black' just like the rest of us. The democrats have ineffectively championed the cause of minorities for decades with all sorts of rhetoric and empty promises while not displaying the courage to break through the barriers of discrimination and inequality that has existed in this country for centuries.

Just as we waited for the masters to tell us what to do next during slavery, we are waiting for the government to tell us what to do now. We have not come together to forge a power structure that can sit at the table and demand recognition.

Power never concedes anything without a demand. It never has and it never will.

(Frederick Douglass), (Robinson, 2000)

Those of us who have, give large contributions to charities that then disperse the funds so thin by paying salaries, buying equipment and losing monies to corruption, that your contributions really have little effect, leaving a never-ending cycle of need for your contributions.

There is an old saying that I have heard many old people say that goes like this; "Instead of giving you a piece of my fish, I will give you a pole, teach you how to fish and direct you to the stream and you can get your own fish." Consider this; Instead of each person donating 1 million dollars to a charity, have 5 or 6 people who can afford to donate 1 million dollars come together and build a company that would supply the daily needs of an entire community while at the same time creating jobs for that community, hire the people of that community which will in turn uplift that community. Then we ourselves can build homes in our communities that we can be proud of because we created and built this community up with our own hands.

In a discussion with my 75 year-old mother, she said something that really surprised me. Although my mother has always been pro-black and instilled a sense of black pride in all of her children from very early ages, she was never the revolutionary type. But just recently, while we were talking about the very status of our people, my mother said, with an angry passion; "we have enough people with enough money to create our own cities! It is a shame that our people cannot come together and do something that would really make a difference." This statement comes from someone that grew up during the time of 'Jim Crow' and has struggled for her entire life just to make ends meet. She and my father worked hard everyday and could not even buy their first home until they had reached their forties. I knew that my mother was always concerned about the status of our people, however, I never knew that she had such radical views regarding our progression. I wonder just how many people feel just like her and what happens to those who may have felt that way when growing up but changed once they did become successes. Could it be that we cannot trust each other or is the self-hatred that we were taught as part of our indoctrination into American society still running that strong amongst us?

As small business owners black businessmen have acquired a notorious reputation among our own people. We have lent credence to the term 'CP Time' because we are too casual about professionalism that includes dependability, presentation, efficiency and timeliness. Although I have come across many black business owners who were very professional in their presentation and the execution of their respective practices, I have experienced far too many that didn't. Many small businessman approach their business with a small-minded mentality. They dare to endeavor into self-employment for the soul purpose of being their own boss, neglecting the impact that they could affect if their purpose were more universal. Let us also make note that the lack of self-awareness and self-confidence of the small black business owners is only a part of the problem. A large part of the problem affecting black business is the lack of patronage to black business from black people. The author Carter G. Woodson stated that:

> "The strongest bank in the United States will last only so long as the people will have sufficient confidence in it to

> keep their money there. In fact, the confidence of the people is worth more than money."
>
> (Woodson, 1933)

Dr. Woodson went on further to say;

> *"Yet it is not necessary for the Negro to have more confidence in his own workers than in others. If the Negro would be as fair to his own as he has been to others, this would be all that is necessary to give him a new lease on life and start the trend upward."*
>
> (Woodson, 1933)

No one understands this phenomenon amongst black people more than the foreign element. Foreigners recognize our dilemma the moment they set foot on American soil. They immediately infiltrate our communities and set up shop. They recognize that we will eagerly patronize a white man's business or a foreigner's business before we will patronage a black man's business. We prefer to spend our money elsewhere. We have more confidence in the product and service that someone outside of our race can provide than we do our own. As pointed out earlier, there are several reasons for this occurrence. Here is an example of one other reason small black business fail.

Some years ago there was a corner store in my hometown of Newark, New Jersey. It was an ice cream parlor that also sold a few household items like bread, milk and cigarettes. The black man who owned the store was a very nice and personable young man. He kept a little thirteen-inch television on top of the freezer and there was always some sports on it. We often talked sports whenever I patronized his store. The main things that I mostly brought from his store were cigarettes, a sub sandwich and a milkshake. There was a small supermarket about four doors down that I brought household goods from. One evening I went out to buy cigarettes and found his store closed. So, I went to the other store and found that the cigarettes there were almost sixty-cents cheaper. I was curious about the reason for this disparity, so the next time I went into his store I asked why his cigarettes cost sixty-cents more than the Israeli supermarket.

His reply stunned me. He said, "You're paying for the extra service that I give." I was befuddled at first and then I realized that he was referring to the friendly greeting he gave when you entered his store, the congenial banter that was passed back and forth and of course, the thirteen-inch television on top of the freezer.

Excuse me! I thought those things were called professional courtesy or customer service with the exception of the thirteen-inch TV, which was actually aimed behind the counter so that he could see the game while working. Besides, I got all of that from the Israeli store down the street except for the little TV, which he could have kept that to himself. Needless to say, I did not buy my cigarettes at his store anymore as I then began to notice so many others bought ice cream from him and then went down the street to buy their cigarettes. It is very unfortunate that this particular businessman thought it necessary to charge his patrons extra in order to receive common courtesies in his establishment. All too often, small black businessman attempt to gouge their community and many times provide inadequate service all in favor of gaining a small buck or hustling someone. This is not an overall blanketing statement to stereotype all small business owners. But far too many black people think small; live small and automatically place limits on their own ability expand and grow. Every now and then, an individual whose talents may not be as visible as Michael Jordan's or Beyonces', emerges and rises to soaring heights simply because they thought big, live big and had the foresight to place no limits on what they thought they could do.

We, as a people, must pay special attention to the details. We must take heed of the fact that we already have one strike against us. We must use that as motivation to ensure that we dot all of the I's and cross all of the t's and give our ultimate all to the progression of our endeavors, whatever they may be, and our people. So, I beseech all successful black businessmen to take some time out of your busy schedules and reach back into our communities and lift our children's knowledge of business to another level. I acknowledge that there are many, many programs being performed all over the nation by concerned and conscious individuals. Some are dedicating their lives to bringing awareness and education to the black people of this country and there are also many people who are supporting these programs. That in itself is not the problem. The problem lies in us as a people. We need more people to participate.

The mass as a race is not supporting itself on either end.

The average black layman, while working hard to supply the necessities for his family does not consider the fact that better conditions and unity among his people would automatically mean a better quality of life for his family. In the black community the small business owner's offspring often don't aspire to continue or advance the family business. They don't think of going to college to learn automotive engineering or business management in effort to expand Dad's auto mechanic garage into a full service automotive chain or grandma's grocery store into a box-store supermarket chain. The American educational system does not emphasize these long-range goals among black and minority students and neither does the black family. We must acknowledge that improvements in the status of the blacks in this country will not happen overnight, but rather in the future as those changes will create a better world for our children and their children. Instead we, and our children look for the instant get-rich-quick scheme or a course of more immediate gratification or we simply never look past today's dollar. We, as a people, generally do not pass on businesses or corporations to the next generation. Mom's small beauty shop will rarely, if ever, grow into a one-stop health spa featuring hair care, skin care, a massage therapist and a gym with certified professionals, on-site medical staff and nutritionists.

The generations before us made great sacrifices at the risks of their lives to forge what gains we celebrate today. The current conditions of our youth today reflect both our positive activity and our overall inactivity. Malcolm X, at the conclusion of his speech in 1963 at the Abyssinian Baptist Church during a question and answer period was addressed with a member of the church stating:

> *"Look at all the progress we have made since 1865." Malcolm replied, "The only progress we have made is as consumers. We still don't manufacture anything; we still don't legislate for ourselves. Our politics is still controlled by white people, our economy is still controlled by white people, therefore, we have no real say about our future."*
>
> *Malcolm X, (1963)*

There are indeed thousands of young black people forging forward with positive agendas. However, there are more thousands that are being lost everyday. With each generation, the loses are becoming younger and younger. Up to recent years studies have shown that each incoming generation has had the opportunity to achieve greater earning power than the previous generation. A recent study states that in reviewing the future of our economy's progression as it exists today reveals that this trend will change drastically and the next generation of young blacks, for the first time in decades, will not have those opportunities to earn more income than their parents as a whole.

This is very discouraging and for me it paints a very ugly picture of regression. We, as a people, are already chasing and any regressions at all will simply leave us lagging even further behind and make it harder for us to rebound, if just back to where we are. We must jump into action now. We must gather full strength and invest fully in ourselves. We can, bar a full recession, improve the economy within our own communities by buying and creating businesses and investing in property and real estate with a universal goal in mind and not for individual gain alone. In fully investing in these things we can become more self-reliant. As long as we exist in this country we can never be totally independent due to the social structure of this capitalist society. But, we would be able to hold our own and establish a greater amount of control of our lives and our future.

Considering the fact that we have many individuals who have proven that they can compete at virtually any level in science, medicine, business, entertainment and sports, if we could only learn to be of one mind, pursue one universal goal and support our own endeavors, we can compete with the entire world and become a force to be reckoned with. If we could possibly tie into all of the black nations throughout the world and combine the resources, manpower and brainpower of all the people of color, I believe the scale of power will begin to shift into another direction. After all, people of color are the majority on the planet.

I can imagine that as you are reading this you may be saying, "such an idealist." However, if you would look at the world today you would see that there is just a handful of people who dictate the ebb and flow of the entire world. These people, although from different nations, work together to ensure that the wealth and power stays within their realm. So far no one has gathered enough strength to challenge that regime. We as a people must remember and be inspired by the fact that we are the original thinkers, the originators of civilized society and the original warriors and protectors of the planet. Our ancestors once occupied the position of power for thousands of years. Is it so unbelievable that it could and should be returned to the original and true heirs?

We have young men and women making large sums of money conducting illicit businesses like drug dealing and prostitution. The real successful ones have all of the attributes of a CEO or president of some legitimate businesses. They are personable, charismatic, aggressive, ruthless, talented and motivated with business and street smarts. Most of them, however, do not have the confidence in themselves to transfer those skills and talents over into legitimate business.

Today, the most lethal enemy to black owned business is black people themselves. As a whole, black people have a very self-destructive attitude toward themselves. As mentioned over and over throughout this book, this evidence of our indoctrination or orientation into this country. We were taught not to support one another in our everyday lives, let alone sacrifice to support one another. Question: Would you walk an extra block or two or drive an extra couple of miles to support a black owned business when there are several white establishments that sell the same thing along the way? Why have we not, as a people, invested seriously in producing and providing products needed in day-to-day life operations? Instead of supporting farmers by buying other peoples products, we should be employing our own farmers to produce our own products. History tells us that we are the original farmers and keepers of the earth. People of color inhabit the most fertile and productive lands on this planet. Our ancestors taught the European how to farm. Why are we not monopolizing in this area?

A young, well-established basketball star, in a November 12, 2005 interview on ESPN with sports commentator Steven Smith divulged that he pledged one million dollars to the victims of Hurricane Katrina. He also took the time to fly down to the Astro Dome where many of the victims were being housed and offered help with the issues that were going on down there. Those things are very commendable. This same athlete went on to announce his own company; an auto specialty company that 'pimps-out' high end SUVs for those who can afford it. Now, there is nothing wrong with creating an income producing business that caters to a target customer. However, if we all thought more in terms of the evolution of our people, would it not be more advantageous for a person in a position to institute a lucrative business, to institute a business that would produce products that we need to survive and jobs for citizens of a given community? It seems that we have a grasp on the need for power, prestige and wealth, but we are not conscious of the needs of our people as a whole. How many black people can afford to trick-out their SUV (not saying that they don't do it anyway) and do those who can really need to do it? How many televisions does one need in his or her vehicle and what practical purpose does spinners on a wheel have? We have the game truly twisted. We pursue individual riches and material 'stuff' instead of people power, political power and true independence as a race.

An ex-homeless playwright hits it big and achieves a great deal of success with his plays. He buys a multi-million dollar home with 27 rooms. How many homeless brothers and sisters did he take with him and, if he indeed took any, was it enough? We endeavor in movie theaters, production companies, sports teams, casinos and vehicle enhancement services. Not one of these endeavors provides a necessary and much needed product or service for our communities, nor do they generate much employment opportunity or positive return to the community. Many of these companies, indeed, bring in substantial profits from within the respective communities in which they operate, but how much are they returning back into that community? The main service that most of them provide is some sort of entertainment, which is not an absolute necessity like milk, food or soap and also, again, does not provide many local job opportunities. Therefore, on the surface it just seems that these businesses simply take from the community while putting very little back.

Looking at the same situation from a different and more objective viewpoint reveals other, behind the scenes, benefits created by such endeavors, many of which are still disconnected from the communities in which they operate. For example, a movie theater provides a venue

If Not Now, When?

for new directors and actors to showcase their talents, which in turn provides job opportunities for production crews, engineers and other related positions. But, in my opinion, this is like taking from Peter-to-Pay-Paul. Taking from the community in which it operates while putting nothing back and providing employment opportunities (a relatively small amount) from outside of that community is self-defeating.

The problem here lies in us being objective. This is the time for us to be subjective. We, as a mass of people, need to be more concerned with ourselves, and our state of existence here in the United States, as well as all over the world. We have contributed amazing amounts of resources to every aspect of existence on this planet, yet we are still considered as, and treated as second-class citizens. Even in the recent winter Olympics, a young black man, Shani Davis, made true history in being the first black man to win a gold medal in the winter games and it was over-shadowed by meaningless controversy regarding team misunderstandings. Many of their superstars and top prospects failed to bring home the gold. Another participant and teammate was unable to participate in the remaining portion of the games due to the fact that he was sent back to the States for getting into a drunken fight in a bar that involved the local police. Was that not more controversial and embarrassing? Young Mr. Davis should have been exuberantly celebrated for clotting the bleeding of embarrassment.

In order to reclaim our rightful place as true Kings and Queens and the original caretakers of this planet, we must first proclaim our independence and freedom.

X.
Respect:

The early tribes of the planet had great respect for Mother Nature and the natural flow of the universe. They respected her beauty and power and they feared her wrath and destructive capability. So, life back then was shaped around Mother Nature's natural cycles. There were contingency plans for the rainy season and preparations for the uncompromising dry season and even the hurricane seasons. All three were opposite extremes, but those tribes survived Mother Nature's cycles through respect.

Today, the word 'respect' has evolved into a transparent or translucent state. The word has become 'thin-skinned' and can be easily torn. Although the word is still used, there is very little commitment to it. Modern man is getting further and further away from truly respecting Mother Nature and the natural flow of the universe. In the past naturalist and scientist alike taught us that all things are relative. For instance, first off everything grows old and dies making way for the new. Vegetation grows unregulated, so deer and the like eat the vegetation and multiply at a steady pace causing an over population. Lions and other predators eat the deer, thus thinning or regulating the herd and finally man kills the lion and then dies from old age, consumption, disease and natural disaster, again, making way for the new. This is a very simplified version of natural attrition.

Well, modern man is constantly searching for ways to subvert that natural flow. They keep trying to create barriers and structures that would control or protect against Mother Nature's will. They are aggressively pursuing artificial methods of creating life by cloning or some other 'sci-fi experiment. I sometimes wonder if they (scientist) seriously think that they can duplicate God's work and not experience serious consequences; or are those consequences already factored into their efforts.

Anyway, this blatant disrespect for Mother Nature and the natural flow of the universe has translated down into the everyday lives of the world's inhabitants. As I had mentioned earlier in this book, there is a growing disrespect and lack of commitment to the word of GOD, the act of love, manhood, womanhood, marriage and brotherhood. These are all things that are natural to the Homo sapiens. All that man does today is against his nature. Let us look at life today. We are destroying the ozone layer which helps protect us from harmful ultraviolet rays, we have provoked global warming which is steadily changing the face of our planet, we are polluting the air and the water, and we are stripping the planet of its resources. There is more disease and mental illness, more deviance and maliciousness than ever before.

For those of us who believe in the bible and the Word of GOD, all of the signs are revealing themselves daily. For those of us who don't believe, and base all conclusions strictly on science, you cannot deny that at this rate the inhabitants of this planet are devolving into inhumane and uncaring savages and the planet itself will soon self-destruct from the abuse and neglect. The powers-that-be consider industrialization as the only means of progression. The perfection of the soul, spiritual nirvana and a more humane connection with mankind through brotherhood does not bare promise for as much material gain. If that is indeed your case and you believe in the 'The Big Bang Theory', you may very well get to see it close up and personal.

Man has learned many things about the human psyche and although there is much, much more to learn, he has gathered much

If Not Now, When?

information about why we do some of the things we do. Yet, with all of that knowledge we still promote actions that result in negative reaction. Let me explain in a little more detail. Many studies have shown the great impact of television in regards to its influence on the human brain. Too many times have I been watching some sappy, tearjerker movie and found myself smiling genuinely at some heart-warming scene. I always catch myself and ask, "what the hell am I smiling about, it is only a movie. It is not real." For a few moments I was lost in that scene and it was subconsciously very real to me.

Let us put the innocent mind of a child in that same scenario. The little one has just come home from school and mommy is watching her daily soap opera. There is a scene on at 2:30pm in the afternoon with two people writhing, moaning and kissing passionately in the bed. A switch to another scene with two people arguing with one actor shouting, "you'll pay for this, you crazy bitch", and in reply the other actor says, "you bastard, when I finish with you, they will throw the book at your ass." These are everyday scenes and dialogues that you can find on many different shows from dramas, to adventures, to comedy, at any given time of the day. To this child this is real. So there is no wonder that children are cursing out adults using words that we never even thought of using back when Lucy and Desi could not even sleep in the same bed on television. There is a no-holds-barred attitude and just about everything goes. In following the 'letter of the law' we have forsaken morality and ethics. This is the foundation for chaos. There is a growing lack of respect for parenting, civility and morality. Oh, it is talked about in speeches and presentations, but the actions of this society show something totally different. The conspiracy theorist in me smells something else brewing. In observing the deterioration of morality and ethics in our society, and, at the same time, the direction that our government is creeping, I see evidence of a pattern. The impending chaos is the perfect excuse for big government to ease deeper and deeper into our private lives. This is all too evident in the actions of our government especially within the last ten years. Take the Terry Schiavo case or abortion rights. Should the government be able to dictate how you live and die or how and when you choose to die? Should government be so deeply involved in, or pass laws and judgment on what a woman does with her body? Then we have the

'Patriot Act' which in no uncertain terms legalizes the invasion of privacy and now the emergence of 'closed-door policy making' and 'eminent domain', which gives government the ability to confiscate personal property for commercial business. These are the signs of 'Big Brother' emerging from his closet in preparation of overseeing every aspect of our lives. It begs the question; Are these occurrences to be thought of as 'Controlled Chaos'?

Another example of this 'Controlled Chaos' is the popularity of 'Gansta Rap'. The big-time promotion of 'weed-smokin', 'gun totin', womanizing, liquor drinking young black men and women who inspire violence and negativity while gaining maximum visibility. Two of the most popular icons of this phenomenon are 'Snoop Dog' and '50-Cent'. Both of these young men present negative images, yet they have been allowed to enter into mainstream American life. The images being promoted by these and others like them help to keep the minds of our youth on the verge of chaos constantly. Who, really, are these people who would totally flip out on the two second display of one of Janet Jackson's breast, but sit quietly while Snoop Dog viciously kills people in a video game and '50-Cent makes a mainstream movie called "Get Rich or Die"? I believe that 'Big Brother' wants our communities on the verge of chaos. Maybe that is why there are so many liquor licenses given out in the urban areas. In any urban setting or minority community, you will find a bar on every other corner and in between them is a liquor store. A drunken mind is a mind in chaos.

I hope that I am raising some questions in your minds. If you keep our warriors drunken and ignorant we can never gather an army to oppose the tyranny of the oppressor. The President of the United States has depended on a certain level of chaos. This level of chaos has kept us distracted with mis-directional tactics and has constantly deflected focus from the real issues. From the infamous "weapons of mass deception/destruction", to the ill-chosen 'house seat' choices, there has always been some sort of distraction from the real issue of the day. The 'powers-that-be' have always known just how to distract us. Basically, by sending someone that looks like us into our mist to divide our loyalties. As stated earlier, there is power in numbers. Even the most basic creatures on our planet instinctively know that. They travel in packs, herds, prides, flocks, armies, gaggles and schools. Predators instinctively know that the easiest way to take down a prey is to divide the group, break down the numbers with surprise and chaos, separate the chosen subject and capture and destroy them, one by one.

United we stand, divided we fall.

This is the way the black man has been dealt with from his initial arrival in this country. In fact, this is the way the black man has been treated all over the world.

XI.
AIDS:

There is a scourge among us. Although this scourge attacks all peoples without any disparity of race or color, it is affecting our people disproportionately. The spread of infection in the countries of people of color surpasses the damage and death toll of the bubonic plague of the 12th century when access to medical care was virtually non-existent. Now, with medical breakthroughs in the treatment of the HIV/AIDS infection, this important medical treatment cannot seem to find its way to those countries with the most devastating infection rates, which happen to be inhabited by people of color.

In this country alone the numbers are too alarming to ignore. In a recent report in the Atlanta Journal Constitution in November, 2005, Dr. Ron Valdiserri, the acting director of the CDC's National Center for HIV, STD and TB Prevention, said,

> *"New HIV diagnoses continue to disproportionately and severely impact African-Americans, both men and women. We must remember the human impact behind these numbers and continue to work together to reduce this glaring disparity."*

Atlanta Journal Constitution, (November 2005)

Personally, I take offense to the simple fact that Dr. Valdiserri found it necessary, even if subconsciously, to remind the world of the human impact. Not because I am accusing the Doctor of being racist, rather because the world's view of people of color dictated the necessity to remind the world that we are a part of the Human Race.

Also, in the same article, the CDC reported that although there has been some reduction among individual groups, there has been no meaningful reduction among HIV's most common victims; racial minorities and homosexuals. The CDC's Dr. Lisa Lee reported, "African Americans account for an incredible 51% of all new diagnosis and have a diagnosis rate of 8.4 times higher than whites. New York City accounted for more than 20% of all HIV diagnoses in the CDC study." Dr. Carlos Del Rio, a HIV researcher and professor of Medicine and Infectious Disease at the Emory University School of Medicine in Atlanta, Ga., in his research separate from the CDC study, said,

"Rates among African Americans are incredibly high."

The CDC study also reveals that men who have sex with other men have accounted for 44% of all new diagnoses and a recent showing of rise in syphilis for the fourth straight year supports those increasing HIV numbers. (AJC, November 2005)

Now, for the world-view; in an astoundingly compelling statement submitted to the book, "Pandemic: Facing AIDS", Kofi Anan, the Secretary General of the United Nations had this to say,

"In twenty short years, HIV has spread to every corner of the earth. Over sixty million people have already been infected, and of those, more than twenty-five million have died. In the ten countries most severely affected by AIDS – all of them in Africa – a fifteen year-old boy today has more than 50% chance of becoming infected with HIV at some point in his life and, in due course, dying of AIDS.

There are forty-six countries around world, in Africa, Asia, Latin America and the Caribbean, where at least one in forty pregnant women is infected with HIV. In the worst affected

places, more than a third of pregnant women have been found to have HIV. Everyday, more than 2000 children are born with it, even though the world has the tools – through drugs and quality pre-natal care – to make the transmission of HIV from mother-to-child a rarity.

The impact of AIDS in individuals and families is mirrored by its impact on economies and societies. Adults in the prime of their working lives are stricken and their productive skills are lost. The security of communities is under threat, as a generation of young people grows up without adequate adult guidance, nurturing, care, or love. The loss of every breadwinner's income makes it harder for his or her dependants to obtain health care, education and nutrition, thus leaving them more vulnerable to infection. This cycle need be repeated only a few times and AIDS destroys an entire community."

Kofi Anan, Secretary General of The United Nations

Have we not grabbed your attention yet? Is this information not poking through to your heart, soul and brain? Is this scourge not yet knocking at your door, touching someone in your tribe, or maybe even you? This information is not just reflecting how I feel about the scourge of AIDS, it is scientific fact provided by the top researchers and scientist in the field today. Researching this information was very traumatic for me. It awakened and electrified three major emotions in me; anger, sadness and despair. The book "Pandemic-Facing AIDS" was jolting. It is a must read. It brings the stories of courage in the face hopelessness and reality to the nightmare that is HIV/AIDS. HIV/AIDS is a scourge on the verge of surpassing epidemic proportion.

If not now, when? When will we learn that if we do not take care of our own that no one else will?

HIV/AIDS has touched my life, striking down at least two people in my own tribe who were very close to me and several friends and associates. It changed my life, my way of thinking and my destiny. If this disease has not affected your life in any direct way, although unfortunate, but I must say, at this rate, it will. The only thing that we can do is stay consistent in taking all possible precaution to prevent it from happening to us.

Interviewing different people, I found several dominant theories regarding the origination of the virus. Many white people that I have talked with contended that the virus originated on the continent of Africa through some mutated green monkey virus and other white people think that it was an experiment gone awry and transmitted to Africa by a gay sailor. Many people from many different cultures and nationalities view this pandemic from a religious standpoint. They contend that the virus is a plague sent from God to punish all of the sinners and backsliders of the world. Some believe that God is preparing us for 'Judgment Day' and others believe that God is simply cleansing the world.

Most 'conspiracy theorists' swear that the HIV/AIDS virus is a man-made weapon aimed at people of color and homosexuals. In the 1987 edition of Health Consciousness an article by Dr. William C. Douglass entitled "WHO Murdered Africa" detailed some very disturbing evidence that the World Health Organization (WHO), along with our government ordered the creation of this disease and it's deployment. In his article, Dr. Douglass contends that,

> *"A 'New World Order', in its attempt to control the planet, has in effect, created a method of controlling the population of the world. He states, "The World Health Organization in published articles, called for scientists to work with these deadly agents and attempt to make a hybrid virus that would be deadly to humans. In the bulletin of the World Health Organization, (WHO), Volume 47, p.259, 1972, they said, "An attempt should be made to see if viruses can in fact exert selective effects on immune function. The possibility should be looked into that the immune response to the virus itself may be impaired if the infecting virus damages, more or less selectively, the cell responding to the virus."*

The viruses mentioned in the above statement are the bovine leukaemia virus (BLV), which is lethal to cows and the sheep visna virus, which is lethal in sheep, neither of which is lethal to man. Both of these particular viruses are called 'retro viruses', "meaning that they can change the genetic composition of cells that they enter."

The original story released by the government claimed that a native African was bitten by an infected green monkey and thus began the spread of the AIDS virus in Africa. Dr. Douglass goes on to state,

> "Virologists know that the AIDS virus doesn't occur naturally in monkeys. In fact it doesn't occur naturally in any animal."

In another controversial research paper conducted by Dr. Theodore Strecker called 'The Strecker Memorandum', Dr. Strecker wrote,

> "In the early 1970's a high ranking government official (of which he named) wrote a top secret document—a National Security Memorandum ("NSM 200") – in which he indicated that "depopulation should be the highest priority of U.S. foreign policy towards the Third World."

Dr. Strecker goes on to state,

> "This memorandum which can be obtained from the U.S. National Archives, which was only declassified very quietly in 1990, was adopted by the National Security Council as official U.S. foreign policy towards the Third World."

Both Doctors contend that several all too obvious and incredible coincidences occurred just prior to the massive outbreak of the AIDS virus. Dr. Douglass writes,

> "The World Health Organization went into Central Africa in 1972, into an area that is now known as the "Aids Belt" and administered a smallpox vaccination to several thousands of Africans." In 1972 there was the first outbreak of the AIDS virus in Africa, followed closely by other Third World countries.

Dr. Strecker, in his memorandum, states,

> "The AIDS virus didn't exist in the United States before 1978."

Dr. Douglass contends,

> *"Another startling fact that was never mentioned in the mainstream media - the Hepatitis B Vaccine that was given to several thousand male homosexuals in New York and San Francisco. The fact is, every single person who received that vaccine contracted AIDS – every single one of them, without exception. That is what the first American victims of AIDS all had in common. They were receivers of the Hepatitis B Vaccine. It is documented fact that AIDS began in America in the homosexual communities of New York and San Francisco immediately following a 1978 government sponsored program of Hepatitis B Vaccinations."*

Now, although it has been alleged that this information has been 'blackballed' from mainstream media and publication, it is obtainable and many people know of these documents and these accusations. I contend that whether it has been substantiated as true or not, if it has not been substantiated as not true, then we as people of color should be in a 'state of rebellion'. Immeasurable efforts should be taking place as I write these words to find out the truth. Our leaders should be going to prison and risking assassination in their efforts to uncover these documents, if they indeed exist. Also note, that whether it is true or not, the effects are indisputable. Our people are dying by the millions.

All of the changes that I have called for throughout this book will act as weapons against the spread of this disease. When a people begins to have more pride in themselves and believe in themselves and really begin to believe in their God, they may be less likely to abuse their bodies and expose themselves to eminent death by partaking in such risky and destructive lifestyles. This is not just idealistic mumbo-jumbo. Do some research and look into other countries that are still steeped deep into their ancient cultures, traditions and religions versus countries that have been infiltrated, colonized and or enslaved and had another religion forced upon them. The differences are too obvious to ignore.

The Vatican City is set in solid gold trim with golden door knobs and priceless art and the Pope sits on a bejeweled throne, yet the largest groups of their followers are in the Third World countries being ravaged by HIV/AIDS. As stated earlier, the necessary drugs and the money to battle this disease has not been made available to the countries most desperately in need of them. The Catholic Diocese is one of, if not, the most lucrative and longest existing businesses in the history of the world.

We should be taking this personally. Collectively we, as a people, have the resources to create our own research centers and hospitals. We have experts who have ascended to the pentacle of every field in existence and entrepreneurs who have amassed great individual fortunes, and another truth is that there are many white people who have, throughout history, helped us and even risked their lives in the name of humanity and justice for all.

This killer discriminates not between religions, political affiliations, or personal beliefs. Can we not overcome the indoctrinations and trainings of the slave masters of centuries past? Can we not overcome the psychological slavery that has permeated throughout our race even after the physical chains of bondage have been removed? What would it take for us to put aside our petty differences and band together for a simple and basic cause called survival. Brother Na'im Akbar in his 1991 book, "Visions for Black Men" queried this particular subject. He supposed,

> *Just imagine where we would be if DuBois and Garvey could have gotten together. Just imagine where we might be if Dubois and Booker T. could have gotten together. Just suppose Elijah Muhammad and Martin Luther King, Jr. could have gotten beyond those surface differences that separated them and united their skills for the salvation of our people. What if Elijah and Martin could have sat down together and Elijah would have said, "Let's do something for ourselves," and King would have replied, "We shall overcome!" If they could have held hands and taken off they could have really changed Chicago, changed Atlanta and changed America. Our communities are weaker today because these great and powerful minds could not come together. How powerful we would be now if Jesse Jackson and Farrakhan could have stayed together after they came together. Our leaders must come together. It can only be done when those people who take on the responsibility of*

> *leadership have initially taken on the mentality of a "man" which does not get blinded by deceptive divisiveness."*
>
> *(Akbar, N. 1991)*

Here is a cry out to all religious leaders of all denominations and nationalities. Put aside your religious differences and your power struggles. It is time to petition for the salvation of mankind. We see on a daily basis the fortunes that have been amassed by our religious leaders from Minister Farrakhan to Bishop Eddie Long to Crefelo Dollar and T.D. Jakes, just to name a few. These men hold incredible power bases individually and are all men of God. Whatever you may title that all-encompassing entity, if you truly believe in him, then you should believe that he is the master of all and we are all his children. While individual fortunes are being amassed on a daily basis, so are the deaths of tens of thousands of African and African American children.

If so many of you can rally up your congregations against homosexuality and same-sex unions at the behest of the leader of this country and the extreme religious right, then indeed you can rally up your congregations of thousands against the killer of God's children. We need hospitals that will concentrate on our problems. Together with the medical, scientific, business, entertainment and sports fields we should be sacrificing to create our own research facilities, hospitals and hospices in effort to take care of our own and to deal with the world issues that affect us disproportionately. The individual power-bases of all of these 'Religious leaders' are very impressive to us, but to the powers-that-be, they are of no threat or significance.

The exact same goes for all of our successful business entrepreneurs, entertainment moguls and super-smart scientist, researchers and doctors, top sports icons and other high profile, successful individuals; individually, your accomplishments are impressive to the people who support and follow you, read and celebrate in your successes. But individually, you are of no threat to those who run the world. You all bear little weight in the destructive way the world is being controlled.

As mentioned several times earlier in this book, scientists have made great strides in controlling or inhibiting the effects of the HIV/

AIDS virus, yet, the places that are hardest hit and being ravaged by this plague are places inhabited by people of color and they are not receiving these medications. Why is that so?

Do people of color not count? Is it simply an issue of money? After all these countries are very poor countries. Or, is there really a conspiracy to rid the world of all the unwanted unworthy races? How can we claim a moral majority in this, the richest country in the world, when we sit back and watch as disease, war and genocide rampage through countries too poor to defend themselves? How do we claim the title "The Police of the World" and only intervene when there is some profit to us?

When I say 'us' I am referring to Americans. Yes, I am an American. Sometimes I am ashamed of that fact, but the truth is that the only people more American than black people here in this country are the American Indians. This country was built from the blood, sweat and tears of our races. The American Indian was tricked and massacred almost into extinction. The African was brought here as slaves and built the foundation of this country with bare hands and bended backs. All others immigrated here of their own free will thinking that they were coming to the promise land.

> *"Your country? How came it yours? Before the Pilgrims landed we were here. Here we have brought our three gifts and mingled them with yours: a gift of story and song – soft, stirring melody in an ill-harmonized and unmelodious land; the gift of sweat and brawn to beat back the wilderness, conquer the soil and lay the foundations of this vast economic empire two hundred years earlier than your weak hands could have done it; the third, a gift of the Spirit."*
>
> *W.E.B. Dubois, The Souls of Black Folk, 1903*

The Americans see, but they don't see all of the wrong and destruction being executed on a daily basis. If not now, when?

When will we wake up from this nightmare and correct all the wrongs that have been perpetrated against our people. When will we see that they have experimented on us before, (The Tuskegee Experiment and The Venereal Disease, Gonorrhea and Syphilis experiments in Africa) why wouldn't they do it again? When will we fight back?

XII.
The 'Invisible Enemy':

One would think that our most formidable enemy would be the HIV/AIDS Virus or one that we can see but can't seem to defeat, like the white oppressors of the world. But that is not the case today. Our vulnerabilities to those foe have now become only the causal casualties of another enemy; 'The invisible enemy'.

Our invisible enemy is only invisible to us. Everyone else sees him very clearly. He can move freely among us without ever being detected. He is in all of the places that we are. He is invisible because he is us.

The Invisible Enemy

I see the invisible enemy, there's one outside my door

Even this side my castle gate, there's two or three or four

They walk our walk; they talk our talk, and love our women true

They lead our children to the well, but first they drain that too

I see the invisible enemy; he wears his pants like me

We praise his style, but all the while, his snipes we just can't see

But each snipe is right on target; each assault does mark its goal

Since we see no wounds of flesh and blood, we forget to check the soul

I see the invisible enemy, but most my brothers can't

They're the ones who sing "Black Unity!" to the tune of a mindless chant

You don't see him right here among us, at school, at home, at work

You don't feel the evil presence, of he who sits and lurks

I see the invisible enemy, as he grows with each day past

As he smiles and says, "I hear you bro", while he steadily kicks my ass

I see the invisible enemy, and I'll rip his cloak and mask

And make him see that he's only me, looking in the looking glass."

Linwood S. Hancock

    I once had a supervisor many years ago who picked on me constantly. He yelled and screamed at the slightest little mistake. He made a habit of embarrassing and degrading me in front of other workers and vendors. It took all that I had to keep from punching his lights out. This supervisor was a small framed middle-aged black man with a booming voice. Needless to say that every time he chastised me everyone heard it.

    One particular day, when I had endured about as much of this abuse as I could, I went to his office with my resignation in hand. Before handing him my resignation, I asked what was the problem

If Not Now, When?

he had with me or what did I do to make him dislike me so much. His reply stunned me. He said, "I do like you boy. You are a good worker. I was just trying to teach you how to make it in this world." I asked him, "What exactly was the lesson that I was suppose to learn from your constant abuse?" He answered, "I was trying to teach you tolerance, boy. You young guys are always so angry and ya'll always ready to fly off the handle."

I stared this man straight in the eye and stated sternly, "I don't want to learn tolerance to abuse and I will always strike back at anyone who attempts to abuse me. If you wanted to teach me something, you should have taught me how to be professional and be the best machine operator in the plant."

We, as a people, have been far too tolerant of abuse for far too many years. The Rev. Dr. Martin Luther King learned that tolerance will only get you so far. At the time when he began to spit more fire in his speeches and address more controversial subject matter, his young life was snuffed out. One of the ways that the 'Lynch Letter' is still affecting us is through how and what we teach our young people. If we teach them tolerance of wrongdoing, then they will grow meek. If we teach them to stay within the parameters of what we know, then they will be limited. We must teach them to 'loose' their spirit and let their minds and hearts run free. If we teach them right from wrong and its penalties and give them structure and responsibility, that freedom will turn into constructive accomplishment. This is evident in the many young adults that are achieving great goals and fighting the good fight today, but they need help.

We must not allow our children to sit mindlessly in front of a television set or video game without structure or time constraints. We must force them to use their imaginations. We must teach our young people to think freely and to allow their imaginations to flow, but at the same time we must teach them discipline and give them a foundation based on structure. Freethinking and flowing imagination without discipline and structure can result in chaos.

The intentions of the supervisor at the beginning of this section were honorable and he meant well, however, these are not the times for tolerance. It is also not the time for mindlessly striking out. We must teach our young people the difference between a battle and the war. But we must not teach them to be meek and subservient. They need to learn what battles to forgo in order to have enough strength and energy to finish the war.

Here's a hypothetical situation: An upcoming bright and courageous new young leader emerges on the political front. He gains ground quickly as he champions for the betterment of his people. He is one of the few non-religious leaders with the courage to speak out and rally the people for the cause. Right at the height of his crusade, he is assassinated. How do we, the people, react? We are hurt and outraged. History dictates that we will riot in protest. That is our normal pattern to such a tragic event. The problem is we rage in our own communities, destroying what little quality of life we have. We revolt by burning, looting and pillaging our neighbors and the businesses that serve our communities. When it is all said and done, our new leader is still gone and no one has been prepped to fill his shoes. Worst yet, our neighborhoods look like burned out war zones. Our children have to step over debris and blood in the streets in route to school. Finally, we have to start all over again rebuilding, and some things will never get rebuilt and are lost forever. Sound familiar.

We are indeed our own enemy. Far too many of us will sell-out for financial gain or forget where they come from once they have reached "financial security". We become content with donating to some charitable organization, which is tax deductible, and go happily on our way feeling justified. Just recently it was reported that the Red Cross is being investigated for misappropriation of funds and corruption. I wonder exactly how much of your donation really reached the people that needed it most? We spend so much time and energy pursuing capitalistic goals that we forget the villages of our humble beginnings. This goes for those who have descended from slavery as well as those who did not. We have all descended from Africa. We place blame on the less privileged and poor as if they are purely poor on purpose. We fail to take into consideration the ongoing psychological ramifications of slavery and how it affects us all very differently. We fail to realize that we still own or control very little when it comes to a world-view. The very bottom line is that in a country where your skin color is representative of your humanness, you are still a 'nigger'; the difference is that you are just a 'nigger' with money. You may be considered a smart nigger or a special nigger, but a nigger nonetheless.

I once worked for a large pharmaceutical company back in the late eighties and early nineties. I served as an administrative assistant and was the only black person in my entire department. I got along famously with everyone that I came in contact with at that company, which was mostly because of my mother's teachings that I was as good as anybody and her constant reinforcement of pride in our identity, and my experiences in the U.S. Navy during the Vietnam War where I was exposed to, and lived in close quarters with many different races and nationalities under stressful circumstances. In any event, all of my coworkers treated me kindly and with respect until they found out that I was from Newark, New Jersey. Many of them had traveled through Newark in route to Newark International Airport or Penn Station and witnessed the substandard way of life that exists in the ghetto. They listened to the local news reports of the crime, drugs, illiteracy and desperation that manifest itself within ghetto life. The discovery of my origins changed their outlook of me. No, they did not treat me worst or disrespectfully, in fact they seemed amazed. They were surprised that I spoke so clearly and expressed myself with such civility both orally and through written expression. That said to me that no matter what my personal accomplishments or experiences were, the fact that I was black and from the ghetto dictated to them that I was some sort of anomaly. "Oh, you speak so well," or "You don't carry yourself as if you were from Newark." Are we ignorant to the fact that in the eyes of the majority, that although we may be respected for our abilities, that we had to rise above our natural blackness, exceed their expectations and perceptions and become better than black? It is simply not the same as it is with a white person who succeeds or achieves. That is expected, and he or she deserves credit strictly for their talent. We, on the other hand, are an unexpected surprise and a credit to a race that is not expected to achieve such heights. And, it never fails, that once one of our achievers commits a negative (human) act, he or she is then acting as is expected. If you don't believe me, ask O.J. Finally, many of us adapt those exact expectations of those of us less fortunate than others and consequently look down on our own kind.

We react to injustice with blind rage and chaos, leaving ourselves open for infiltration, sabotage and division. We are like the sports team that is packed and stacked with the greatest superstars in the game, but they can't come together to win a championship. Oh yes, we have many bright stars and brilliant minds in our midst. However, we can't come together to uniformly fight for a just and righteous cause. The 'powers-that-be' are brilliant strategist. What they lack in numbers, they compensate with long term planning and trickery. Our uncontrolled emotions and leaderless ploy leave us victim to that trickery every time.

We, as a people, all too easily, self-destruct our own accomplishments. We whine about our own use of the word 'Nigga' when that word no longer has the power that it once held. In today's world with all that we have accomplished in every field, we subvert those accomplishments by taking offense to the use of that one word by some ignorant 'Redneck'. When that word is used publicly by some hateful racist who has no other means of attack, we want to protest and demand an apology. What we should be doing is ignoring him/her and teaching them just what a so-called 'Nigga' is capable of. We should be concentrating on those who are smart enough not to say it out loud, but shows how they feel in their actions that affect us covertly.

Our so-called representatives come out of the woodwork whenever someone says something negative about our people. They hold press conferences and attempt moratoriums against the originator of the insult. But where are they and what are they doing in between the public insults when injustices are occurring every single day to our people all over the world. We should be screaming out everyday. Sometimes I believe that we shoot ourselves in the foot worrying about the small stuff. What we should be concentrating on is the big stuff like reparations. If you want to execute a protest about something, make it something bigger than mere words. Make it something that will benefit us as a people. Jewish people demanded and received reparations for the Holocaust. Japanese people received reparations for the treatment they received here in the U.S. during World War II. Did you know that if you can prove undisputedly that you are at minimum one eighth Pequot Indian that you will receive a residual check from the casinos.

Every so often someone brings it up and asks for some sort of compensation. It has yet to work. When will we, as a group, learn to demand our due.

> *"Power never concedes anything without a demand. It never has and it never will."*
>
> *Frederick Douglass*

When will we learn that great achievement means great sacrifice? We must be willing to sacrifice some of the luxuries that have pacified us for so long in effort to achieve that goal of equality that we have longed for even longer. I believe that we must digress back to the fifties and sixties when the civil rights movement was strong and effective. There was a sense of unity and community. Sit-ins and boycotts were the flavor of the times. It was a time for action. With that mindset for activism and the financial and political power that we have achieved to date, we should be able to make some major changes in, not only this society, but significant changes throughout the world.

XIII.
Black on Black Crime:

I have heard people say, "Why should there be a statistic on black on black crime? Every race commit crimes against its own people. Criminals don't really discriminate, they just hit the easiest target. They usually work within their own environment."

Well, for those of you who feel that way, I agree with you 100 percent. You are very right in your assessment. However, the answer to your question of 'why' is very easily answered.

In the history of the entire world, no people have ever suffered the subjugation and degradation, as a race, for as long and as completely as our people. Therefore, we cannot consider ourselves on the same playing field as everyone else. Our situation does not fit any of the graphs or measurements used to gauge the activity, growth or lack thereof, of any other people. We are on a more difficult level with obstacles of greater significance and because the playing field of life is so uneven, we are set at a definitive disadvantage.

However, despite this acute disadvantage, we have shown sustained flashes of brilliance and certain levels of superiority. As mentioned earlier in this book, we have provided samples of our capabilities all throughout history by achieving unsurpassed levels of excellence in virtually every field in existence. This information is confirmable and public knowledge and record available to anyone who wishes to enhance their awareness of black achievement and invention.

Acknowledging this disadvantage should, by all rights, inspire us to unify and wage a nationwide or even world-wide campaign against any and all who even attempt to hinder our forward progress. To avenge, or at least, right the wrongs done to our people should be at the top of our priority list. Because we were beaten down and segregated, not only from mainstream society, but also even from ourselves, we should be pulling together with an extra energy in effort to reverse the effects of that segregation.

People, on all sides of any given issue, use statistics and studies in many different ways. Different sides of a particular issue can take the exact same study and interpret the results in totally different ways; ways that would support their particular point of view. I use the statistics of 'Black on Black Crime' to support my theory on the effects of the self-hatred and division that was emblazoned into the minds of the Black American Slave. Those statistics serve as a visual aid. I have yet to find statistics on the light-skinned versus dark-skinned internal wars between black people, but we all have seen them in action in our everyday lives. Have you never heard a black man say, " She is too black for me," or a black woman say, "I hate a light-skinned man." Seeing and receiving, and acknowledging and taking action are two very different events. A person can see something everyday for years and never really acknowledge its existence.

We must not be blinded to the injustices, nor should we allow ourselves to be consumed by them. We must learn to see, receive, acknowledge and take action against any and every system or person who attempts to divert us from our destiny. We must also learn to see, acknowledge and take action on any and every opportunity that would enhance our progress and unity. We must begin to acknowledge and then act upon who, what and where we are and from where we come respectively, and begin our quest from there. I think that once we create a universal unity that defeats the concepts of the 'house Negro' versus the 'field negro', the light-skinned Negro versus the dark-skinned Negro, and the Black man versus the Negro, period, there would be very little that could hinder our progress in both mind and state. Remember, knowing is only half the battle.

Now, with that said, with such rich history and ancestry, with an established reputation of unstoppable resolve, staying power and determination, what, pray-tell, could possibly hold us back. We are no longer subject to public whippings and executions; we are no longer banned from reading and learning or forced to work under inhuman conditions; we have access to great sources of knowledge and the availability to gain access to uncountable amounts of resources and personal freedoms. What force or entity could be so powerful as to render the mass of a race incapable of taking advantage of those opportunities?

Steven Bilko, a South African activist said,

"The most powerful weapon that the oppressor possesses is the mind of the oppressed."

If I may follow up that profound statement with a quote from the renown educator and historian John Henrik Clarke, who stated,

"The only people that can truly end slavery are the slaves...."

"If there is someone on your back, causing you to carry extra weight, the only way to balance or offset that weight is to bend over. The best way to get that extra weight off of your back is to stand straight up."

Although we no longer wear the physical chains of oppression, our minds and emotional state still suffer the consequences of that period of 'Official and Legal Slavery'. Today we suffer from a mental prison created by that period in our history and perpetuated by both a deeply engaged society and our own unwillingness to acknowledge it. This subtle mental state still affects us all, rich and poor, young and old alike.

The force or entity that stifles us today is embedded deep inside of us. We have broken the physical chains, but the mental chains still hold us at bay. Our own minds are our greatest enemy. The old 'slave mentality' still permeates efficiently through many of the lives of our people. It limits what we think we can do; it limits where we think we can go and it constantly rejuvenates the interracial hatred that was taught during our orientation into this country. We no longer have to be reminded of who we are in this society, we simply remind ourselves by staying in our place and playing the roles that we have been stereotyped into.

I am compelled to repeat a quote used early in this book by Dr. Carter G. Woodson,

> *"When you control a man's thinking you do not have to worry about his actions. You do not have to tell him not to stand here or go yonder. He will find his 'proper place' and will stay in it. You do not need to send him to the back door. He will go without being told. In fact, if there is no back door, he will cut one for his special benefit. His education makes it necessary."*
>
> *Dr. Carter G. Woodson, 1933*

The challenge that confronts us is not an easy one to defeat. A civil war against an enemy who looks different from us would be so much easier. Once war is declared, you strike out at anyone who doesn't look like you or wear the same uniform as you. That would seem simple enough. Unfortunately, that is just not the case in this situation. How do you identify the enemy when he wears the same uniform as you; he looks, walks, talks and knows your weaknesses, just like you do and sometimes better.

However, when the revolution comes, our enemy will be revealed to us in subtle ways when we all jump into action. He will be the one less willing to sacrifice and go that extra mile for victory. Our enemy is not just a sell-out. He could simply be the 'stand-by' brother; the ones who stand by and watch others achieve and progress and then looks to share the spoils of victory. Or, he could be the old 'slave-minded' type of brother who refuses to do anything against the master out of fear and/or loyalty. Our enemy will come with many excuses and we must be diligent in recognizing them. Before we can achieve true unity and greatness as a people, we must defeat and eradicate our worst and most formidable enemy; the enemy within.

XIV.
To My People:

This is not a blessing out. It is a cry out. I am not placing blame. I am simply pointing out the facts as I see them. The fact is that we must attack the deficiencies within our own people. We must overcome the psychological damage that has rendered us victim still, but first we must acknowledge that damage. Both, rich and poor, educated and uneducated alike, must acknowledge that we have grown more and more distant from one another for more serious reasons than wealth and academics. Our plight is still the same, although we may intimate them in different ways.

This book is also an acknowledgment of recognition for my transgressions. I have been guilty of many of the things that I have eluded to in this book, therefore I speak from a standpoint of someone who has spent many years in blindness just as have many of you. I was awakened some years ago and decided to clean up my life and concentrate on something bigger than myself. I was reawakened at the occurrence of Hurricane Katrina. She reminded me of things that I already knew, but was too busy to address.

This book is part history lesson. Throughout the book I cite some specific events and important people in our history. But most important of all, I hope that I have incited some of you to research and study our history on your own. All of my life I have been searching out historical facts about the greatness of my people and I am still searching and learning more and more everyday. What I find is that the more I learn about myself the prouder I become and it shows in my walk, my attitude and my resolve.

This book is a challenge to all people. I challenge everyone to change, including myself and join in the 'Revolution for the Evolution of Black People'. We need the participation of our entire race in acknowledging and taking actions against our own individual faults and weaknesses, and against our true enemies. I truly believe that the uplifting of the Black race will improve the human standard all over the world.

This book is part search for religious truth. If all people of the world were taught the real truth, maybe many of them would accept the true magnitude of the connection between us all. The only thing that separates us as human beings is geography. Each and every one of our histories intertwine and evolve from one true origin. We are all the children of God. The real truth about the origin of religion would reveal the true connection between white people and black people all over the world. We are all of the same cloth and we are all brothers and sisters in the eyes of the Father.

It is truly going to take the cooperation of the entire world, white, black, yellow, brown and red to save our planet from the destruction that the human race has incurred. But, it is going to take the original caretakers of the planet to bring everyone else back to their senses and back to a more natural way of life. We, my people, are the original caretakers and keepers of the planet. Think about it; nowhere in the world is there more fertile soil, more growth and vegetation than in Africa and South America, where scientists believe the two were once one big continent. If you examine Africa and South America, you can see how they fit together like puzzle pieces. In fact, if you examine the entire planet and all of its landmasses, you will see that they all fit together as would pieces of a great puzzle. This lays credence to the theory that man wandered from his place of origin, traveled across greats masses of land, settled, colonized and set the stage for what is the world and its many races and nationalities today.

Although evolutionists and creationists may disagree on the evolution of man, many of them do agree on the origin of the races.

If Not Now, When?

It is scientific fact the climate and geographic environment dictate skin pigmentation, hair color and textures along with other physical traits such as size and body structure. All of which changed and adapted to its geographical surroundings over the generations into the many different races of today. Many evolutionists and creationists also agree that the origin of man is in Africa.

The amount of melanin in a person's system and its reaction to the environment and exposure to the intensity of the sun dictates the color of that person's skin. The varying intensity of the exposure of any person to the sun determines whether that person will be dark brown, black, yellow, pink or white. The actual color of melanin varies between a reddish color to a dark brown or black color. Human beings indigenous to the more tropical regions or areas closest to the equator, therefore closest to the sun, are naturally darker skinned. Human beings indigenous to the colder regions or areas farthest from the sun are lighter and sometimes almost white.

Now let's review these last few paragraphs. Both evolutionists and creationists, scientists and theologians believe that man originated in Africa. They both acknowledge the effects of the sun on the chemical melanin made naturally by the human body. They both believe that tribes from long ago either wandered or were exiled to different parts of the world where they settled and spawned generations who then adapted to their environments.

What does this tell you?

If God created man in His own image and that man is from Africa……..?

One of the things that the paragraphs above should tell you is that there is only one race; the human race. Once you peel away the many layers of skin you find we all look exactly alike. All of the differences are superficial. We all laugh, cry, love, hate, feel pain, bleed, pee and die alike.

Recently, I visited the Atlanta Civic Center to see the exhibit entitled, "Bodies". An artist ingeniously preserved human bodies and displayed them from "bone to skin". Every muscle, artery, vein, ligament and organ was shown in its natural position and how it functions. It was an amazing display and extremely educational. It also revealed how much we are all alike despite the differences in our exterior appearances.

XV.
Community

There have actually been many instances where black people have raised strong, stable and successful communities. I have referred to many of them earlier in this book. There was the most famous one, Rosewood, Florida. This story was depicted in a movie starring Ving Rhames and John Voight and told the tale of a small community of ex-slaves and other black immigrants who came together and created a home for themselves. Rosewood is one of many communities that grew up during the time of Jim Crow and they all shared the same fate. A community of hard working, law-abiding, God-fearing black folk just trying to survive while making the best of the lie of 40 acres and a mule. But it's fate, like so many other communities during the troubled time surrounding World War I was already forthcoming. Amidst much racial tension, a young white woman claimed 'she had been sexually assaulted by a black man'. The same scenario occurred all over the nation. In fact, during 1919 alone more than two-dozen different race riots were recorded across the nation. This period was an 'any reason will do' period and white racist used many different reasons to burn black communities down to the ground.

These recorded riots were very different from those we know of in the 1960s and the 1990s. These riots were instigated and executed by white mobs, many wearing white hoods, attacking, destroying and burning black communities. In contrast to the more recent riots, which revealed black people rioting over some distinct injustice, the difference was they are burning down their own neighborhoods. Consequently, we, ourselves were the only ones to suffer the backlash of our rioting. The riots of the early century by white racist mobs stopped all normal operation, disrupted government activity and totally dislodged their target victims way and quality of life.

There are two lessons to be learned from this information.

#1. We, as a people, are totally capable of establishing, governing and sustaining a successful community.

#2. The fear of reprisal is so much more deeply entrenched in our psyche and is more severe now than it was 80 years ago. It appears that we are less likely to fight back against our enemies than we were when slavery was fresh on our minds. We have so much more individual materialism to lose at this point.

Those black people who established those communities long ago were more than willing to take up arms to protect those communities. They were just not ready for such a savage onslaught.

Back in the 1960s the Black Panthers and the Nation of Islam attempted to re-establish that community mindset of defending our communities by 'any means necessary'. When our communities began to support their agenda, the 'powers-that-be' jailed and assassinated our leaders. Since then no activist party has raised such controversy for the cause. Today, it seems that we dare not speak out too loudly about the injustices that our people suffer daily, let alone do something that would physically disrupt or affect the daily operations of the perpetrators of those injustices. We could riot. No, I don't think so. The way we riot would just disrupt our own lives. The violators who execute those injustices would just sit on the outskirts of our communities watching us burn them down and restrict us from moving outside those parameters. I have lived through several major riots in my lifetime and in each of them the same format was followed. For several days, minimum if any, law enforcement was present. For several days rioters destroyed, looted

If Not Now, When?

and burned home and businesses. Never once did they leave their own communities. During the 1968 riots in Newark, New Jersey, the authorities placed tanks on the outskirts of the city and watched the destruction for about three days before intervening.

I witnessed the Mayor of Philadelphia burn down an entire city block of residential homes in a black community in an attempt to dislodge one single group called MOVE, a back to Africa organization. Our outcry, and the retribution served were meager compared to the damage that was done. Time and time again injustices are committed against us and our reactions bring only pacification and with that we always quiet down until the next injustice is committed.

One of the communities mentioned earlier in this section was called 'Black Wall Street'. We owned businesses and property there. In the early 1900s we had doctors, lawyers and investors all living in the same community as blacksmiths, grocery store owners, shoe repair shop owners and farmers. Black people owned and lived peacefully in a small metropolis. Today we live in fear inside our own neighborhoods. Not from outsiders, but from ourselves. We can't claim ownership of much of anything within the communities in which we live, so what is there to die for.

The young gangs that terrorize our communities fail to recognize the damage that they truly do. They are killing off and corrupting our strongest warriors. Even Tookie Williams, the late founder of one of the most notorious gangs to date realized the error of his deeds and recanted his evil and violent ways. We are being held hostage in our own homes by that ever-present enemy; ourselves. It is very hard to grow when you are always afraid to step out of your own home. Young gangsters are doing the same job that the Ku Klux Klan used to do. They are killing off our men and raping our women of their dignity, pride and womaness. Worst of all, they are killing and corrupting our youth.

Gangbangers indulge in gang wars over territory that they can never own and a synthetic form of respect that has nothing to do with manhood or humanness. Respect because of fear is much easier to come by than respect because you are all the man, or woman that you can be and simply deserve it. Instead of terrorizing and destroying our communities, gangs should be policing and protecting them. Very,

very few of us have anything deeply vested in our communities, so the attitude seems to be 'nothing ventured, nothing gained', therefore, there appears to be nothing to lose. There is an obvious paradox here. One spectrum sees nothing to lose or be gained by investing in the ghetto, so we live in and accept or adapt to less than desirable conditions. The other spectrum is our young men and women are willing to die for something they will never truly own with the intent to destroy it anyway.

I will reflect back to what my mother used to say many years ago. She said, "Just because you live in the ghetto doesn't mean you have to live like you're in the ghetto." My home as a young boy growing up was always clean, safe and secure. Our floors were always clean and shiny and our furniture was always well kept and lasted a long time. My parents did not tolerate my siblings and I jumping around like crazy people on living room furniture. In other words, outside of our bedrooms or playrooms, we had to, at least, act like we had some sense. Our family didn't have much money and we didn't have a big beautiful home. We were poor, (although I didn't know that then) and lived in the projects (a rose by any other name is still a rose); the ghetto. What we did have was plenty of love, a healthy dose of respect and a solid appreciation for what quality of life we did have. My mother saw that each and every one of us participated in that accomplishment. All of this is to say that although we lived in the midst of the ghetto, inside our home was always an oasis, a place for respite away from the daily strife of ghetto life. I still live by those rules today and they have never failed to improve my quality of life no matter what my surrounding conditions may be.

Very simply if we, as a people, could somehow live by this creed and expand upon it throughout our communities, it would be a good place to start to change our status in this country. Remember this quote by John Henrik Clark:

"The only people that can truly end slavery are the slaves...

If there is someone on your back causing you to carry extra weight, the only way to balance or offset that weight is to bend over. The best way to get that weight off of your back is to stand straight up."

John Henrik Clarke

Many of our people have come home after serving this country in the many wars that plague this country's history and, just like at the abolishment of slavery, faced the big lie. There is no "forty acres and a mule". They can't get jobs, they are offered mediocre medical care and too many of them are left twisting in the wind.

Why can we not take advantage of this opportunity? When these young brothers and sisters return home, they are well trained in a myriad of skills. They have learned everything from hand-to-hand combat, to guerilla warfare; from computer programming to machine operations, auto mechanics and aerodynamics; from military policing to high-level security clearance positions. Are these not the perfect people to protect and support our communities?

Here is a scenario: A group of black people purchases a substantial amount of land and start to build communities (similar to the subdivisions popping up all over the country now). Contained inside these communities or subdivisions would be black owned grocery stores, pharmacies, doctor's offices and lawyer's offices and so on and so on. There would also be some sort of large industrial projects that would help support the community by supplying products much needed by the community and the nation and substantial jobs for the citizens of the community in which it operates. Then we will build a progression of affordable homes for the citizens of these communities. They would range from low-income to upper-middle class.

Along with the rent and/or mortgages, everyone in this community must pay an association fee. This fee would in-turn fund the contracting of an elite, para-military police force that would police and defend that particular community. I am not talking about some militant revolutionaries or some fly-by-night security agency, rather a well- trained, well-equipped, well-disciplined police force that would protect us against our enemies and ourselves. Can we conceive of a centrally-based training facility or facilities run by ex-police and ex-military blacks that would recruit these highly skilled individuals and supply each of these communities with a professional protection force? This force is not to replace the local municipal police, but to work with them lessening their load. The benefit would be that because of the rampant discrimination and racism in the criminal justice system, we would be more or less policing ourselves. Although this would be a great undertaking, I believe that it could work if its implementation is seriously executed. First we must change the way we spend and invest our money.

In a speech in 1963, Malcolm X was quoted as saying,

> *"Anytime the so-called Negro has access to twenty billion dollars a year and you don't find him able to provide job opportunities for himself, this is a sign of sickness".*
>
> *Malcolm X, 1963*

Malcolm goes on to say, as an example;

> *In Long Island the white man bought a city block. On it he built a huge supermarket. It creates job opportunities for about three or four hundred people. Now in the next block, believe it or not, the Negroes got together and bought it and built a million dollar church. Now here this church provides a job only for the preacher; it provides clothing and shelter only for this Negro preacher. Now if this Negro preacher has the ingenuity that it takes to raise a million dollars to finance a million dollar project, but the only thing that he can finance is a church, it's a problem. If you notice, white people in their neighborhoods build factories, they build schools, they build everything, and then they build churches. But the Negro leadership, especially the religious leadership, has actually committed a crime almost by encouraging our people to build churches. But at the same time we never build schools; we never build factories; we never build businesses; we never build housing and things that will solve our problems."*
>
> *(1963 speech by Malcolm X*
>
> *{The End of White World Supremacy, 1971})*

Please keep in mind that Malcolm's statements were made in 1963, over forty years ago! However, we still practice the same methods. If we could somehow divert our energies away from building mega churches and entertainment empires and concentrate on building 'life-sustaining' businesses and independent communities perhaps we can begin to affect significant change to our present predicament.

Consider this strategy: Instead of giving a million dollars to one of America's charities (which always seems like putting a band-aid on a gun shot wound), take that million dollars, pick an urban community and build a new school or buy computers for every student in that school system. Or you could take that million dollars, create a partnership with another million or more and create a 'life-sustaining' business that would provide a needed necessity for survival and provide a substantial number of jobs for the citizens of that community.

The atmosphere of the world today provides the perfect setting for us to make such a move. If we, as a people, should endeavor to succeed at such an undertaking and the powers-that-be create resistance to our progress, then we must let the world (which is already scrutinizing the actions of this nation) know the truth about the "most powerful nation", 'the Police of the World", the "Super Power" called the United States. If we could unify our countless talents, skills and contributions and create an impact on the world as a people, maybe, the world would see the benefit of supporting and encouraging the 'original man', the 'caretaker of the planet', and finally, the most feared man in America.

> *Henry Turner argued in 1904 and refuted most compellingly the charge of inferiority. "More laws have been enacted by the different legislatures of the country, and more judicial decisions have been delivered and proclaimed against this piece of inferiority called Negro than have been issued against any people since time began." Based on the attempts to suppress the race, Turner concluded, "It would appear that the Negro is the greatest man on earth."*
>
> *Allen, Als, Lewis, Litwack, Without Sanctuary, Twin Palms Publishers, 2000)*

To everyone from the Grammy winning recording artists to the lowest level street gang member; from the highest-level government official to the stay-at-home mom; from the preacher to the teacher; from the research scientist to the blue-collar dad and everyone in between; we need you all. We need everyone's participation in effort to make a change. Even if it is something as simple as an attitude change. An attitude change could make all of the difference in the world.

An old man, after spending twenty-five years in prison, once told me that, "There is only one thing in this entire universe that you can control. You cannot control your heart, when it wants to stop, it will. You cannot control what other people do or even what they do to you. You cannot control Mother Nature, whatever she says, goes. The only thing that you can control is your attitude. Your attitude dictates your reaction to acts against your person, your community or your world. How you react determines the true effect of the action taken; whether it be negative or positive. If something negative happens to you and you react in a negative way, the effects of that negative occurrence are doubled because of the repercussions of your negative response. If you react with a positive response, the negative effects are lessened. We must learn to react with a more positive attitude and a purpose, and, we must make our purpose a universal purpose. We should have one unified purpose and pursue one goal. That goal should be justice, fair treatment and respect. Give us that and we will go from there.

Black people here in America have contributed more to this country than any other single nationality, everything from music, thousands of vital inventions, medical discoveries, spirituality, labor, and so on and so on. On the worldwide front, Africa is the mother of all civilization, of medicine, of science, of architecture. Africa was the mother-lode for diamonds and other precious stones and metals like gold. African Art changed the face of traditional European art and influenced art around the world. Celebrated European explorers found evidence that African travelers had already been in all of the places that they were said to have 'discovered'.

Do we not deserve justice, fair treatment and respect?

Genocide and AIDS have been ravaging Africa for many years now and the United States deemed it necessary to intervene in Iraq

If Not Now, When?

where the death toll was minute compared to the death toll in Rwanda and Darfur alone. We must no longer accept second-class treatment and we must rise to the task of taking care of ourselves, both at home and abroad. The only way to accomplish this task is to begin a network of trust between all black people all over the world. We must learn to respect one another before we can expect it from others. We must repair the broken images of American blacks that black people in other countries see.

How in the world do we do that?

Well, without a doubt, it will be a painstaking process. But, we have no time to waste. Everything that we are trying to accomplish must start in the exact same place; inside each and every one of us. Each and every one of us must really, I mean really, look at ourselves in the mirror and ask very simply, "Who am I and what is my worth?"

The history of man, not African history, Black history or world history; the history of man himself tells us that we are the descendants of the greatest rulers and warriors to ever exist on this planet. We are directly connected to the original caretakers of the earth. We are the obvious heirs to the throne. With that knowledge alone, you should immediately begin to restructure your existence. No longer should you accept living in poverty. If you live in the ghetto, you may not be able to change where you live, but you can definitely change how you live. Think about it. If enough people in any given community decide to make individual positive and constructive changes, it could change the state of that entire community, one family at a time.

Picture yourself saying, "I am sick and tired of looking at this old beat up house. This house is not representative of my worth. So, instead of going out this weekend or spending unnecessary money on some things that I can do without, I am going to save some money and go buy some paint and some grass and flower seeds. I am going to paint my house (even if I can only afford to paint the front for now) and clean my yard and plant grass and flowers. This house will begin to show the worth and resolve of the person that lives here. It will show that this person refuses to lie down and simply accept the worst. It will show that this person has the ability to take anything and make it better."

If you are a person who already has access to better resources and finances; if you are a person who gives to different charities, then try giving to a cause where you get to see immediate results. Pick a neighborhood, a city block or the old community that you grew up in (whichever is in the worst shape) and claim it as your pet project. Donate some paint, throw a block-party, organize a 'clean-and-green' project. Get the children involved by cleaning up and planting grass and flowers in unsightly lots. Sponsor free self-help clinics/classes on home improvement by using a home in need of repair within the community. Hold a lottery within that community to help pick the house. Help bring the community together. Help the community to realize that even though the quality of the community may not increase, the cost to live there will. The people need to understand that it is their quality of life at stake here, no matter who owns the property. The people of our communities must come to understand that it is their own responsibilities to better themselves and their individual worlds. We must teach each other that power comes with numbers. If a 'slumlord' is neglecting his proprietal duties, then the entire neighborhood should petition the courts to address him/her. Hell, if that doesn't work, call the 'I' team at 'Eye-Witness' news. Do whatever it takes, but do it together in numbers. You see, no one is watching out for us, not President Bush or Congress. The only real assistance that we will receive in helping us better our status in this country will come from within our own race.

As mentioned earlier in this book, there are many, many black people struggling to be heard and struggling to reach the masses. But the task at hand is just too great for them to be successful alone. The way we can all help out is to look them up. Find local programs in your community and find out what they need. Whether it is small donations of food or money, or it may be volunteers to pass out meals to the homeless or senior citizens, or sit with the children for after-school programs, etc. We must begin to instill a philanthropic attitude in our children so that they can carry on the good fight as if it was a natural part of their daily life.

This is a call to kick-start this revolution. I am reaching out to my generation and the now adult generations that followed me to declare revolution today! We must raise our children as revolutionaries. Teach them that they are natural-born warriors and that they are to take 'no-shorts'. We must declare 'war' on illiteracy and ignorance, on poverty and discrimination and the racism and genocide that we inflict upon ourselves. I have read many articles and witnessed evidence of how we are still, here in the 21st century, being erased from history. I have heard and read about arguments that one of the greatest warriors in history, the great Hannibal, was not a black man and that the beautiful Cleopatra was Greek despite the thick trail of African blood that ran through her veins.

There have been debates regarding the historical and present inhabitants of northern Africa and how they are not of African descent. I have spoken with some black Americans who believe that the present-day ruling class of South Africa and Australia are the indigenous people of those regions. The lack of knowledge of African history amongst our own people is astounding.

We need authors, historians and movie producers to produce historically correct movies about the world's greatest kings and queens. Huge epics like 'Ben-Hur' of the past and 'Gladiator' and 'Troy' of the present, need to done about Hannibal and Pilhanky, 'The Pious', and many, many other great black warriors. Here is an idea for an exciting action-packed epic movie; 'The life of a black warrior/queen, Queen Qudit or A Kentakee, who was actually a female Pharaoh. There are fantastic tales of love, romance and conquest to be found in our history and we must bring that history to our people just as every other race has done. Let us take those tales out of the books and out of folklore and place them in a medium that we know we all enjoy; movies. Although they stirred up much controversy, we all made concerted effort to see 'Mandingo', 'Shaka Zulu' and 'Roots'. Those movies involved our encounters with the white man. The best of our history occurred centuries before his dominance ever came into existence.

History and religion has been tailored and contoured so much that as more and more bits of truth eek their way out into the main stream, great debates have been sparked regarding which history is really true. It is our responsibility, as the descendants of such rich ancestry, to reach out and discover the lives, adventures and contributions of our existence on this earth. It is our responsibility, each and every one of us, to strike out and find our truth. We have been fed someone else's truths for hundreds of years. We must wean our children away from 'His-Story' and introduce them to 'Our-Story. The bare truth is that the white race does not have a history without us, but we do have a history without him. We, black people, were everywhere that people existed from the beginning, the white race made history invading and conquering.

Conclusion:

This book is meant to uplift, support and incite my people. It is imperative that my people hold themselves and be held by others, in the highest esteem possible. The most powerful society today was built on the backs of my people, as was the very first civilization. I am not trying to tear us down, rather, I am trying to inspire us all to say, "If not now, when? I have also attempted to provide feasible alternatives, solutions and actions that we might take in effort to viably combat the conditions that plague us today. For decades we have complained about the treatment we receive and about the way we are looked down upon. For years we have beaten up on ourselves in attempts to figure out what to do, which way to turn and where to start without causing too much controversy.

Within the contents of this book, I have suggested many ways that we, as a people, can take to begin to reconstruct our goals and begin to dictate our own destiny. The changes that it would take to start this revolution all begins with the real you; each and every one of you/us. You are a member of a race of people who have dominated in every field in which we have endeavored. The ruling class invented all kinds of competitive games and conspired to keep us out of them. Now we know why. From track and field, all the way to hockey, we rate among the top participants, if not the best the world has ever seen. Did you know that one of the top goalies in hockey is a black man. This is not to say that there have not been many, many tremendously talented athletes that are white, but they did not endure discrimination and degradation while trying to do what they loved. They were not barred from playing or practicing their craft until the last several decades. They were not forced to make up the ground that we have been forced to cover. Not only have we covered tremendous ground, we have surpassed every expectation and to top that off, we are getting better, stronger and faster with each new generation.

The likes of Jack Johnson, Joe Louis, Muhammad Ali, Sugar Ray Leonard, Marvelous Marvin Hagler, Mike Tyson, Roy Jones and Bernard Hopkins have dominated the boxing world for a century. Jackie Robinson, Willie Mays, Roberto Clemente, Vida Blue, Hank Aaron, Ken Griffey Jr. and Barry Bonds are all household names in the world of baseball. Then there is Bill Russell, Wilt Chamberlain, Oscar Robertson, Moses Malone, Magic Johnson, Michael Jordan, Shaquille O'Neal, Kobe Bryant and now, the 'King', Lebron James who have all reinvented the game of basketball. Do the names, Jesse Owens, Wilma Rudolph, Arthur Ashe, Michael Johnson, Venus and Serena Williams, Tiger Woods, Pele, Edwin Moses, Cheryl Swoops and Lala Ali ring any bells. How about Vonetta Flowers winning a gold medal in bobsledding in the 2002 Olympics and most recently, Cornell Jones, the black swimmer, who helped the Americans break the world record in the relay swimming races of the 2006 summer games. Let us not forget the likes of Jim Brown, O.J. Simpson, Bo Jackson, Lawrence Taylor, Reggie White, Walter Payton, and now the tumultuous Terrell Owens dominating the gridiron. The list is endless.

Let's take a look at the movies and theater industry, another area that we were denied entry for many, many years. Before you read any further, I'd like for you to just name, out loud, some of the biggest box office draws and winners of numerous acclaim and awards of today. Samuel L. Jackson, Morgan Freeman, Will Smith, Denzel Washington, Halle Berry, Angela Bassett, Sanaa Latham, Felicia Rashad and the multi-talented Jamie Fox, all following the footsteps of people like Ozzie Davis and Ruby Dee, Brock Peters, Sidney

Portier, Dorothy Dandridge, Lena Horne, Dianne Carroll and Cicely Tyson, in adding color, spirit and soul to the stage and big screen.

The music industry, business, entertainment industry and medical industry are no less packed with talented, powerful and spirited brothers and sisters dominating in their particular fields.

We have in the past, and are still inventing things of tremendous value to this society, from the medical field to the scientific field to the practical household utensil. There have been those who have asked, "What's the big deal?" Many different races of people have representatives in all of those fields." My reply to that question is this: What is one of the first things that an Irish American, Italian, Jewish or Asian American tells you about their immigrant ancestors? "My great, great, grandfather came to this country with thirty-seven dollars in his pocket and a will to work. We have owned our family business for seventy-five years." Well, my great, great, great grandfather came here long before many of yours did and he came with only chains and shackles around their necks, hands and feet and weren't allowed to indulge in free enterprise. Therefore, whatever gains my people have made, they made despite more sufferings and obstacles than any other people in the entire world."

The year 2005 has been a tragic year for people all over the world with an unprecedented number of catastrophic earthquakes, fires, the tsunami, and the horrible string of hurricanes, especially Katrina. The death toll of these natural disasters has been astronomical. Add to those deaths, the death tolls of the genocidal slaughters in Darfur, Sudan and Uganda and the starvation in Zimbabwe and Southern Africa and the thousands dying daily throughout the third-world countries and all over the world from AIDS, and let us not forget the War in Iraq.

Also during the year 2005, many of the icons from my generation have passed on and that fact has brought my mortality to the forefront of my consciousness.

Many times we get lost in the triumphs and struggles of life and we simply forget or just don't think about the fact that we won't be here on earth forever. I, personally, probably have less time ahead of me than I have behind me. The deaths of Ozzie Davis, Luther Vandross, Barry White, Johnny Carson, Eugene Record (Chi-lites), Richard Pryor, David Jennings (News Caster), Christopher Reeves

(Superman), Rosa Parks, Loretta Scott King, Nipsy Russell, August Wilson, Dr. C. Delores Tucker and many, many more all have put me on notice that many of the people who actually witnessed the original civil-rights movement and the atrocities that led up to it are swiftly dying off. Soon, the memories of that era of revolution and activism will be just that; memories. Soon, the soul of the 'struggle' will no longer be alive in the hearts of those who suffered through those days of turmoil.

If we, as a people, don't emphatically reveal 'Our-story' to our children and institute a foundation of revolution as a natural state of mind, then we will leave them victims of 'His-story' and his accounts of the events of our struggle. Although our struggle continues, we are losing more and more warriors to the pacification of material gain. As time passes, the struggle is no longer a struggle for the betterment of our people in a world that has proven hostile to the soul of the black man. Rather, the struggle is swiftly becoming a struggle for individual achievement and perfect assimilation into a world that was not meant for us in the first place. Today we are leading our children into a spiritless and soulless existence in a spiritless and soulless world.

No longer is my wish to leave a legacy of struggle behind. I want to leave a legacy of change: a legacy of completion. I do not want my grandchildren to say that we simply opened doors to opportunity; I want them to shout that we kicked the doors off of the hinges never to be closed again. Our ancestors opened many, many doors for us. We must commit to taking full advantage of their sacrifices and go even further. We must not settle for pacification. It must be all or nothing. We must demand change and if the powers-that-be cannot give it to us, then we must create it. If they refuse to give it to us, we must take it. There is no time left for compromise. There is no guarantee that there will be a third, fourth or fifth generation after us. Nuclear war is impending and Mother Nature is warning, or should I say threatening.

Depraved indifference is like a cancer attaching itself to everyday life with gorilla glue. The crimes against mankind perpetrated by mankind are getting more and more heinous every year. Morality and ethics are steadily deteriorating and our children are the latest victims. I believe in an earthly presence that casts judgment on us daily and it is not GOD and it is not Judge Judy. It is simply the soul. You can call it your conscience or spirit if you would like. I call it the place where your true heart lives. It is where all the lessons of life are stored. Like the lessons of right and wrong, the lessons of compassion, empathy, mercy and brotherly love.

If we don't recapture the true essence of ourselves, we will be totally consumed by the plague and the self-hatred, and negative judgment of ourselves will condemn us far worse than any other source possibly could. If you don't see it, then you are not looking closely enough at yourself and your surroundings. The self-hatred and misjudgment of ourselves is creating more 'Invisible Enemies' everyday. Many people in this country have learned to override the lessons and warnings of the soul. Some act as if they don't even have one, but we all have one. Even if there is no GOD, there must still be something that connects us all together. We, meaning all of humankind, all have too many things alike. Our very existence is like we all came from one organism and simply mutated into different colors, shapes and sizes. How does a huge flock of birds know to all change direction at the same time? How does an army of thousands of ants know what to do to accomplish one monstrous task? There is an innate connection amongst their species and they are all tuned into their own universe. They naturally work together to do what they need to do to survive. Maybe, just maybe, that is the advantage in not having such a large and complicated brain.

There is a natural order to the existence of life in this universe. A flower grows, blooms, pollinates and then dies to make room for a new flower to bloom. Human beings follow in this same order. However, man is attempting to push Mother Nature to unnatural extents and she is rebelling with supernatural force. I pray that before I become a casualty of the war between man, Mother Nature and the universe that I am able to affect some change for the betterment of mankind. In the world today, peace of mind is a fleeting and evasive state. There is unprecedented violence all over the world and the pursuit of quality in one's life can only be guaranteed behind one's individual door. But just imagine if entire communities all decided to pursue that same goal. It would be like that flock of birds all changing direction at the same time or that army of ants all working together in harmony for one universal goal.

Yes, I am the same idealist that I was when I began writing this book. My ideals, pursuits and goals have not dwindled or changed one bit. I am still the eternal optimist despite all of the negativity that I see in the world today. I still see our future as a glass half full and not half empty. My heart is broken each and every time I witness another injustice perpetrated against the human spirit and my soul is diminished every time I see that another black man, woman or child has gone against his nature and viscously taken a life for reasons not involving the survival of his or her own life. We should not take lives whether randomly, maliciously or religiously. Instead, we should only inspire the genesis of all living things. We must revise our definition. America should not define us. We were in existence long before America was ever even a concept, let alone a reality.

We must travel back in time for our true definition. Once we have realized our true greatness, then we must understand and revisit every event in our existence all the way up to today. Only then will we have a better understanding of why we are still here and still going strong. Our reconstruction can then be completed.

It is indeed time for a new definition to describe the Black American experience and we should be the ones to deliver that definition to the world. We should not allow President Bush or Congress or any government to define us. It is time for us to make a stand and make the world take notice. We must inform the world of what is coming: The New Black Man is coming and he is even greater and more powerful than the original Black Man.

Although looking at the statistics and conditions of the black man here in America and all over the world may be discouraging, I am confident that the original keepers of this planet can and will recapture their rightful place. I will never give up hope and I am always ready for the revolution to begin. So, my brothers and sisters…..

If not now, when?

"We are Americans, not only by birth and by citizenship, but by our political ideals, our language, our religion. Farther than that, our Americanism does not go. At that point, we are Negroes, members of a vast historic race that from the very dawn of creation has slept, but half awakening in the dark forests of its African fatherland. We are the first fruits of this new nation, the harbinger of that black to-morrow which is yet destined to soften the whiteness of the Teutonic to-day. We are that people whose subtle sense of song has given America its only American music, its only American fairy tales, its only touch of pathos and humor amid its mad money-getting plutocracy. As such, it is our duty to conserve our physical powers, our intellectual endowments, our spiritual ideals; as a race we must strive by race organization, by race solidarity, by race unity to the realization of that broader humanity which freely recognizes differences in men, but sternly deprecates inequality in their opportunities of development."

W.E.B. Dubois, The Souls of Black Folk, 1903

Autobiography

Linwood S. Hancock was born in Newark, New Jersey in 1956. He experienced the discrimination and race riots of the 1960s and the assassinations of President Kennedy, Robert Kennedy and our beloved Malcolm X and Martin Luther King. He stood as an angry teenager with fist raised along side the Black Panther Party and watched the disenfranchisement of the black man in America after the Civil Rights Movement faded into history.

However, the teachings of his mother and father, the examples of his two brothers and their untimely deaths and his will to learn more about himself and his true origins brought him out of a life that has claimed many of his friends and associates. Linwood spent over a decade working with prison inmates in a rehabilitative capacity trying to change the destructive state of mind of today's young men of all colors, cultures and nationalities. Today, Linwood is married and residing in the Metro-Atlanta area of Georgia and attending college in pursuit of degrees in Criminal Justice Administration and

Early Childhood Education. His goal is to reach as many souls as possible with his message and helping young parents realize that reaching our children at younger ages with positive lessons and discipline is the only way to affect change to this damaged world.

Summary

This book represents my search of the anti-venom that will reverse the effects of that venomous snakebite called racism. The effects of racism and discrimination are still, today, coursing through our bloodstream and because there are no outward or surface wounds we sometimes tend to forget or even deny their presence or existence.

So I speak to the common man, for it is only through us that the necessary changes must originate. I am not angry at the white race; they did what they needed to do to survive in a world where they found themselves to be the minority. This book is not about slavery and what the white man did to us, rather it is about who and where we are now and what we need to do in order to change our state of being.

This book is designed to invoke controversy and conversation, to inspire movement and change and to instill self-pride and dignity to a once-great people now lost.

Linwood S. Hancock II

References

Woodson, C.G. (1933). *The Mis-Education of the Negro:* The Associated Publishers

Robinson, R. (2000). *The Debt: What America Owes to Blacks:* Dutton, Penguin Group

Marable, Mullings & Wood. (2002). *Freedom:* New York, Phaidon Press Inc.

Richardson, N. & Kennedy, R. (2003). *Pandemic-Facing AIDS,* France, Umbrage Books

Akbar, N. (1991). *Visions for Black Men:* Florida, Mind Productions

West, C. (2004) *Democracy Matters:* New York, The Penquin Press

West, C. (1993) *Race Matters:* Boston, Beacon Press

Kunjufu, J. (1985). *Countering the Conspiracy To Destroy Black Boys:* Chicago, African American Images

Kunjufu, J. (1986). *Countering the Conspiracy To Destroy Black Boys II:* Chicago, African American Images

Kunjufu, J. (1990). *Countering the Conspiracy To Destroy Black Boys III:* Chicago, African American Images

Washington, B.T. (1997). *Up From Slavery, The Autobiography of Booker T. Washington:* Carol Publishing Group

Imam Karim, B. (1971). *The End of White World Supremacy-Four Speeches by Malcolm X:* New York, Arcade Publishing, Inc.

Madhubuti, H.R. (1991). *Black Men-Obsolete, Single, Dangerous?:* Chicago, Third World Press

Dyson, M.E. (2005). *Is Bill Cosby Right? (Or Has The Black Middle Class Lost Its Mind):* New York, Basic Civitas Books

Smiley, T. (2006). *The Covenant:* Chicago, Third World Press

Du Bois, W.E.B. (1903) *The Souls of Black Folk:* Edited by Henry Louis Gates Jr and Terri Hume Oliver (1999), New York, W.W. Norton & Company

Cone, James H. (1969), *Black Theology and Black Power:* New York, Seabury Press

Allen, James. (2000), *Without Sanctuary:* New York: Twin Palms Publishers

Stupid in America. (2005). (Television Program) ABC, 20/20- January 2005

William Lynch Speech of 1712, www.thetalkingdrum.com

Medical Information, Homosexuality, www.cmf.org.uk

Human Skin Color, http://www.en.wikipedia.org/wiki/skincolor

The Strecker Memorandum, Dr. Theodore Strecker: www.trinicenter.com

The Strecker Memorandum, Dr. Robert Strecker: www.onlinejournal.com

*African Kings &Queens (*www.blackamerica.com*)*

Skin Pigmentation and Melanin: http://anthro.palomar.edu/adapt/adapt_4.htm

The Origin of Race, www.bible-truth.org/race.htm

Printed in the United States
69391LVS00002B/103-198